THE CELEBRANT

THE CLERGYMAN

THE CELEBRANT

A Novel by Charles Turner

WIPF & STOCK · Eugene, Oregon

Wipf and Stock Publishers
199 W 8th Ave, Suite 3
Eugene, OR 97401

The Celebrant
A Novel by Charles Turner
By Turner, Charles
Softcover ISBN-13: 978-1-7252-5707-8
Hardcover ISBN-13: 978-1-7252-5708-5
eBook ISBN-13: 978-1-7252-5709-2

Publication date 5/28/2020
Previously published by Servant Publications, 1982

To Bob Oliver

ACKNOWLEDGEMENTS

The author gratefully acknowledges
the assistance of:

The Reverend Canon George A. Fox,
Historiographer of the Diocese of Tennessee

Bette Ray Callow,
Archivist of the Cathedral
St. Mary's Cathedral
Memphis, Tennessee

Delanie Ross and the entire staff,
The Memphis Room
Memphis and Shelby County Public Library
Memphis, Tennessee

Trudy Mignery,
Archivist
The University of the South
Sewanee, Tennessee

John J. Heaney,
Church Historian
Church of the Holy Innocents
Hoboken, New Jersey

THIS NOVEL is based on fact. The characters, all but a few minor ones, bear their historical names. Fiction has been employed only for the purpose of bringing the story to life.

·1878·

PROLOGUE

"COURAGE," Father Benson said. "God has a place for you. He will lead you to it."

"But He led me here. I was sure of it."

"I believe that. You must understand, God does not always lead in a straight line. Perhaps He led you here to prepare you further for the priestly office to which you have been called. These three months in England have been with purpose."

"It is quite confusing," Louis said.

"I have no doubt that your calling is to be a secular priest. Life in a monastery is not for everybody. As you know, many of our communion are against it for anyone. We Anglicans have our problems, don't we? Yes. It is good to know that you—wherever God leads—are in heart with us at Cowley St. John."

"I plead with you, give me another chance. My health will improve."

"I'm sorry, Louis. It would be unwise for you to remain. I reached my decision through intense prayer. It is settled. Now, before you go, do you remember what you told me the first day, when I asked what you most desired? You reflected for a long time and then you said—"

Father Benson waited.

"A closer union with Christ."

3

"Ah—and that is not geographical, my son. The bond can be nourished anywhere. Christ is not contained within these walls. He lives in the parishes, too. Remember that. But who knows? It might be that God has a *singular* mission for a young man of your sincerity."

·PART ONE·

·1·

THE ROOM had a bare look. Louis found the spirit pleasant. He thought he might feel at home here. The bed, the clothes press, the ladder-back chair—what more did he need? Maybe he could arrange for an old writing table and, if he sent home for his books, a little shelf.

"You will have a fresh collar every morning, I'll see to that," Mrs. Moffat said.

"I'm not very presentable," Louis said, embarrassed.

"Nonsense. But you must get used to me. I mother every priest who comes along." With hardly a flutter Mrs. Moffat proceeded to point out that a jar was under the bed, and that the closet was two doors down the corridor. Then, leaving, she turned to him again. "You do look so young, my dear," she said, and there was a moment and she was gone.

Louis opened the travelling bag. On top, in a nest of his underdrawers, lay his shaving mirror. He brought it forth and paused to study his face. He did not appear so young to himself. He was twenty-six, and he thought he showed every year of it. If he grew a beard—but no, he had tried that. The hair on his face grew thinly, in patches, and was light in color. He had decided that he looked more mature without it.

He took his time and stowed each item separately and neatly in the press. A sense of settling down—of dropping anchor, of once more being in place himself—came over him, and when he had finished unpacking he stood at the window and drank of the view.

Across the way was the Church of the Holy Innocents, where, starting tomorrow, he was to assist the Rector, the Reverend Mr. Sword. Although the chapel was small, it climbed steeply above the Hoboken street, lending to the neighborhood an adorned and vaulting air. That such a poor section of town should be graced by those Gothic lines did not seem outlandish to Louis. He had heard the story, how the church had been given by the wife of a Hudson River magnate in memory of a beloved daughter. The splendor had been born of a death. He let his thoughts run to theology for a minute or so, until a carriage passing beneath the window caught his attention. Even then his thoughts held the same ascent. Somehow, for him, the action of the horse and the twirls of the afternoon sun in the ungleaming spokes pronounced the glory of God as strongly as did the church architecture.

Today was the thirty-first of August. The heat had lost none of its force, but already the light fell with a different touch. Louis looked forward to autumn. He had learned that failures and worn-out decisions and indecisions were likely to lift and give way to fresh perspectives when autumn cleared the mind. Was it only seven months ago that he had returned from Oxford? It seemed he had carried the disappointment around with him longer than that.

"Mrs. Moffat will fatten you up," Mr. Sword said, passing the dumplings.

Louis hoped the conversation would not get entangled with the matter of his health. Mr. Sword had made it plain that he needed a man who was fit, who was able to work, and Louis had assured him that he was completely over the breakdown. He had improved steadily all spring and summer. Not one spell had he had while supplying at the House of Prayer in Newark during the recent weeks. Please, he thought, let the subject be closed.

He said, "Doesn't she realize that a priest in a poor parish has no business looking well fed?" He meant it mostly as a compliment for the woman beyond the kitchen door.

Mr. Sword said, "You want to get along here, don't you?"

"Very much."

"Then no remarks about my middle."

"Oh, I was not referring—"

He could tell that the fire in Mr. Sword's eyes was pure friendship.

There were only the two of them at table. Louis began to relax and enjoy the company. The Rector was older, a man of dignity—and then a man of bending warmth. Now that Louis thought about it, Mr. Sword reminded him of his father. The comparison tended to make Louis all the more comfortable, for his father was the kindest soul he had ever known. And the truth was, he could share with Mr. Sword one closeness which was not possible with his father, who, though a devout churchman himself, was not as deeply Catholic. At home, in the house in St. Louis, some doctrines and practices could not be discussed without a gentle shifting away, father from son.

"At the altar tomorrow," Mr. Sword was saying, "we shall remember the people in Memphis. Did you see the *Advertiser* today?"

"The yellow fever. It's distressing."

"Five hundred deaths. Seventy in one day. Over a hundred new cases reported. And no hope of letting up before the first frost. At that rate it will prove to be more devastating than in 1873. A short five years it's been. The town scarcely has a chance to get back on its feet before the scourge returns."

"I pray it will not reach St. Louis. They say the poison travels up the river. I'm concerned about my family, naturally."

"We shall remember them, too."

"It would mean much to me."

"God's mercy is to be invoked for the entire region. Memphis weighs heavily on me because our Mr. Parsons is there, has been for two years now. I received a letter from him the other day. He said the situation was dark, indescribable. The stampede is over and those who remained are falling right and left."

Louis, his hunger gone, placed the fork quietly on the plate.

Mrs. Moffat had entered and was lighting the gas. She

said to Louis, "Father Parsons used to be here at Holy Innocents. He was the first Rector, a West Point man who became a soldier of the Cross. *So* loved." She adjusted the flame. She looked at Mr. Sword. "Father, I don't think I could bear it if the fever took him." Her head dipped and she shook it as she retreated.

The halo from the lamp rippled against the thickening dusk. Every surface in the room answered the glow. The walls were in movement with it, slightly, and the talk had caught Louis to a point where he was not conscious of any solid barriers, or of any distance either, between him and the stricken community in the South.

"They can't bury them fast enough," Mr. Sword went on. "And I wonder how many are going to the grave with no service read. Most of the clergy skedaddled the first day, I understand."

"What our Lord must think," Louis said.

"I suppose they have an argument. Human reasoning says that a live minister is more useful than a dead one. Well, I could have told you that Charles Parsons wouldn't turn tail. Or Dr. Harris, with whom he works closely. Dr. Harris is the Dean of St. Mary's. Memphis is a cathedral town, did you know?"

"I had forgotten. I knew that our Sisters ran a school there."

"Parsons mentioned the Sisters in his letter. Remarkable workers. They are called from bedside to bedside, from one end of town to the other. They also have charge of an orphan asylum. Or it could be an infirmary by now."

"I have a great respect for the Society of St. Mary."

Louis leaned forward. "It is inconceivable to me, Father, why some of our brethren opposed the establishment of the order."

The Rector had finished his meal. His gesture with his napkin indicated that he likewise was at a loss, but he let the question go. "Speaking of the Society," he said, "you have been invited to celebrate at the convent on Wednesday morning, and perhaps to supply until the end of the week."

Louis brightened. There was nothing he would rather do than spend a day or two at Peekskill. "With your permission, I would like to accept."

"Of course," Mr. Sword said. And with that, he got up.

"I'm barely unpacked," Louis said, rising, "and I learn that God is sending me off again."

"Not for long, Mr. Schuyler. He knows that I need you here."

Mr. Sword put his hand on Louis's shoulder as they walked toward the common-room. He removed his hand almost as soon as the grasp was secure. Still, a message was delivered. Something in the brief physical contact expressed to Louis the loneliness of past suppers in the clergy-house. Louis knew he was needed for Sunday School calls and to help with the other duties in the parish, and yet he could imagine that he would be appreciated most of all as a presence across the table. A memory of voices came to him. What a contrast between this clergy-house and the rectory in which he grew up. He saw the faces around the table back home. His father loved that circle. And so did he. Louis was inclined to think a priest should not marry, although he had to admit there were many aspects to ponder.

In the common-room the Memphis horror bloomed again. They would drift away from it and then they would drift back. By the time Louis went to bed, the scene of the epidemic had taken possession of him.

He lay awake.

"Would I have turned tail?" he asked the dark.

·2·

AT THE CONVENT, too, the talk was of Memphis.

Sister Constance and Sister Thecla, who had been in Peekskill for a summer rest, had hurriedly "thrown their things together" and returned to the South two weeks ago, at the first report of the fever.

"There was no stopping them," Mother Harriet said.

It was Wednesday and the celebration was over. It was the last of the morning walk. Ahead of Mother Harriet and Louis went the covey of nuns, a wind lapping at their habits.

"But I know you," Louis said. "You wouldn't have kept them from their duty."

"I don't know. I think I was about to try. The danger is so great, even for persons who are acclimated. I'm not convinced the love of Christ demanded their scurrying off to that city of death."

Not a bird cried out. The hill was quiet, save for the breath of wind.

15

Louis clasped his hands behind him. "You will see your children again."

"God knows," Mother Harriet said.

"Yes," Louis said. He felt somewhat reproved.

"And that's what it is—a city of death. I'm beginning to wonder if we shouldn't close the school there, for good. It's hopeless. Every summer is a fear."

Sister Catherine, the youngest of the nuns, had reached the house already and now was heading back along the path, sailing. She skirted the others and they turned with questions in their eyes. Louis saw the telegram in her hand.

"Mother," Sister Catherine said, presenting the envelope.

"What have we?" the Superior said. She sounded drained all of a sudden.

"Good news, I pray."

"And I," Louis said.

Mother Harriet opened the envelope and strolled away, off to herself, to the tree, to read the message. Sister Catherine stood with Louis. Some of the others had started for Mother Harriet, but they stopped short and honored her privacy. The Superior seemed to lose inches from her shoulders while she surrendered to the telegram. When she returned to the group, she managed her posture again.

"It is word from the Sisters of St. Mary in Memphis," she said. "It is not encouraging. The Reverend Dr. Harris is seriously ill with yellow fever."

"The Dean?" Louis asked.

"The Dean."

Someone asked, "What about the Sisters?"

Mother Harriet said, "The Reverend Mr. Parsons also has been stricken."

"No," Louis said. He thought of Mrs. Moffat and her devotion.

"What about the Sisters?" another asked.

"They take no thought of themselves. I suspect that several are down."

Mother Harriet handed the telegram to Louis. He read it for himself. The last line stabbed at him. *There is no other priest of our church in Memphis.*

"They are without the Sacrament," he said.

He found that he was alone.

Mother Harriet was on her way again, angling for the porch. She was in the lead now, hushed, and her wake was a rush of shadows. Louis read the last line again and then walked slowly with his thoughts. The sisters in Memphis needed a priest. And they needed help. People were suffering, people were dying. He felt the Lord's hand upon him. It was as simple and as fixed as that.

As far back as he could remember, Louis had wanted to be a priest. He could remember sitting in the pew, no more than a tot, craning to watch as his father ministered at the altar. He could not deny that in the beginning the desire had been only to do what his father did, and to be like him, in much the way a baker's son might have wanted to invade the bake-shop and smell of yeast and wear flour on his clothes. He could remember the lifted voice and the sermons, and how he had listened and wondered until he drowsed against the silk of his stepmother.

He had attended a school taught by a lady in the parish. He could remember telling her he wanted to be a priest when he grew up—her mouth had made an oval at the announcement—and he could remember that she prodded him with his serious intention whenever he fell into mischief. What arrows her smiles had delivered on those occasions. On Fridays, to prove himself, he never failed to remind her of the catechism lesson. Friday was the day for recitation and Louis Schuyler was always prepared, arm in the air.

And when he was older, a boy of fourteen, he was given charge of his father's horse and carriage. He had considered it a manly duty, and he had liked it. He had hoped it would dispel the idea that he was a delicate, sickly creature. In good weather, and sometimes even when the St. Louis wind cut like a blade of ice, he drove his father on the round of parochial calls. He would take a book along. While his father made a visit, he would sit there in the carriage, waiting, reading, feeling that he too was a servant of the Lord.

Only once had he questioned his long ambition, and that was during his freshman year at Hobart College, when he first began to comprehend the true obligations of a clergyman. He was homesick, and he began to think of the self-denial that would be involved in the life. He went through a wilderness there for a time, searching his motives. How could he be sure that the call was of God and not of his own fancy? The pull he felt toward the beauty and mystery of the altar—was it merely sensual? Did he love God only on the level that he loved the feel of a book in his hands? Did he respond to God only in the way that he responded to a graceful turn in a sonata? If so, he might fail Christ and wither at the demanding responsibilities. He did desire to be of use to the Savior, but did Louis Schuyler have the necessary heart for all the sheep? He had offered up his doubts as if they were supplications. Not for a moment, though, did it seem that God had released him from the plan.

His first full appointment had been at Oak Hill, near St. Louis. It was a struggle, a parish of boisterous families— miners, most of them—and under his care the church had grown. He liked to think that the membership had grown not only in number but in a knowledge of Holy Scripture. How he had tried to instruct that flock. And how he had prayed for them, and for the unbelievers around, that they would be conquered by Christ's love.

He had discovered that a temper for prayer was the steadiest gift he had received from God. When he left Oak Hill and went to the monastery in England, he had not felt that he was dodging the realities of the Christian battle. Not at all. The way he saw it, the case was entirely the opposite.

He still held that opinion, and because he did, the episode at Cowley St. John was as disconcerting as ever. But that was over and he had better let go the past, he told himself.

"Come in," Mother Harriet said, without looking up. She was putting quill to paper.

Louis entered. He placed the telegram on her Prayer Book and said, "I am going to Memphis."

The quill, after the first flourish, scratched to a halt.

Mother Harriet's eyes rose. "Don't be too hasty with such a decision. You haven't had time to fully—"

"Time enough. God was very quick with me." Louis snapped his fingers. "Like that."

"Oh." It was more of a sigh than a word. Mother Harriet stood. She attempted a smile. "I forget the adventures of the young. Forgive me. And God's will be done. But I wonder—"

"Do not wonder about this," Louis said.

"You must consult with Father Sword, of course. Do you think you will have his blessing?"

"I count on it. He is deeply concerned about the situation. Everyone at Holy Innocents is, because of Mr. Parsons."

"I advise you—may I advise you?—to see Dr. Houghton first. Stop in the city and talk with him. He is taking applications from those who are willing to go. It is on *him* to choose. Let *him* say."

She was following Louis into the hall.

"I shall call on Dr. Houghton today," he said. "Let's see, when is the next train?"

"At 9:45."

Louis glanced at the hall clock. It was 9:14.

He said, "If I hasten—"

Sister Catherine was in the door of the altar-bread department. She was not good at masking her interest.

Louis was going for his things. He heard the Superior say calmly to Sister Catherine, "I suppose you know what Father Schuyler has in mind."

·3·

LOUIS SAT in Dr. Houghton's parlor, waiting to present himself. Here, after the sun, was almost a darkness. The room gave the silence of a well. The window was open and the curtains were gathered back, but the atmosphere of the rectory softened the forenoon and mellowed the clip-clops that went by.

He had known the address. East Twenty-Ninth Street, around the corner from Fifth Avenue. The Church of the Transfiguration was a favorite of his. He had walked from the station and he was perspiring. He had planned to stop and call on his brother, Monty, who lived in the city, but he had decided against it. He pulled out the linen handkerchief and mopped at his face and down into his wilted collar. As soon as he stuffed the handkerchief away, he could feel new droplets forming. He blamed his excitement. The day was not all that warm. Respectful of the fine old fabric of the chair, he sat forward as he waited.

Dr. Houghton had gone to the *Times* office with Bishop

Quintard. The housekeeper expected them back shortly. Bishop Quintard was up from Tennessee, seeking aid for the people of Memphis. "He is Father's guest," the housekeeper had said.

Louis was glad to think he would have the opportunity to offer his services directly to the Bishop. He was glad also that it happened he had these minutes to straighten himself and get his breathing right. Eagerness was one thing, nervousness was another. There had to be dignity, a dignity that would speak of strength. He had never met Bishop Quintard and he wanted to measure up as a suitable volunteer.

A gray velvet cat came in from the hall and took stock of him. Louis greeted the cat, but it kept a distance. Louis tried to charm the cat, but it left the room.

On the table beside the chair lay a volume with a worn and handsome binding. Louis picked it up. It was *Henry Esmond,* an old friend. Louis went to a remembered part and lost himself for a whole page. This was the peace of God, he thought, to be able to draw aside and enjoy a bit of Mr. Thackeray at such a time. The occupation did not seem appropriate to the circumstances, however, and he closed the book and placed it on the exact dustless rectangle where it had rested before.

Looking at the ceiling, he began to say The Order for the Burial of the Dead. He used both Psalms. Although he bobbled now and then, he left his Prayer Book in his pocket. He was far into the Lesson when he heard the rectory door push open. He broke off from St. Paul in the middle of a phrase.

Masculine voices, genteel, sober, brought a conversation in from the sidewalk.

Louis stood.

Once the introduction to the Bishop was done, Dr. Houghton said to Louis, "And how have you been getting along since your return from England?"

"I am well and strong," Louis said. He wished to put forward his proposal without ado. "I have come to talk with you about—"

The Rector was informing the Bishop, "Mr. Schuyler was with Father Benson at Cowley for a time last winter."

"Oh? The monastery." It was obvious that Bishop Quintard was held by other matters, yet he did lend attention, more than was comfortable for Louis. "I am very interested in Father Benson's ideas."

"It was a great privilege for me," Louis said.

He preferred not to go into the particulars of his stay at Cowley St. John, for surely would come a discussion of his leaving.

Dr. Houghton said, "Mr. Schuyler is soon to assist Mr. Sword, at Holy Innocents in Hoboken."

"I have already begun. Sunday."

"The weeks go by," the Rector said, "and Memphis has gripped us so. My calendar is not the best."

They were sitting now, the three of them.

The Bishop mentioned that Mr. Charles Parsons had come from Holy Innocents. "To think that he and Dr. Harris both lie in my house today, victims of the fever."

Louis could contain his proposal no longer. "It is in regard to Memphis," he said, "that I have reported here. I want to go, to do what I can to help."

"Your willingness is appreciated," Bishop Quintard said, and he fished inside his coat and produced a little book and a pencil.

"Have you spoken with Mr. Sword?" Dr. Houghton asked.

"No, I was at Peekskill when I heard that the priests were ill. I am returning to Hoboken this afternoon. Mr. Sword will support me, I am confident."

"I'm inclined to believe that he will," Dr. Houghton said, "but we must remind you, Mr. Schuyler, there is much to consider."

"God tells me to go. Is that not the major consideration?"

Dr. Houghton gave the question some thought. "For you, yes. But you see, God has appointed to me a responsibility in this. I pray for rational decisions. It is possible that He is simply testing you for an obedient heart. Perhaps the action itself will not be required of you."

"An obedient heart without an obedient action?"

"Mind you, I don't want to sound like some of our brethren who can sever the physical element until everything is vapor."

Bishop Quintard, having written in his little book, said, "Mr. Schuyler, you *have* taken action. Your coming here today was the proper step of faith. I have listed your name with the others who have volunteered."

"I can be ready to leave tonight."

The Bishop seemed to be putting two and two together. He asked Louis, "Are you the son of Dr. Montgomery Schuyler?"

"Yes, Bishop."

"Christ Church, St. Louis?"

"Yes, Bishop."

"Your father is highly esteemed."

"Thank you. He is highly esteemed by me, certainly."

"Do you think that he would assent to your going?"

Suddenly his father was there, sitting in the chair that had been empty. The paternal gaze was long and deep. Louis began to lose the edge of things.

"It would be difficult for him. But my father would never ask me to disobey God."

"Tell me," Dr. Houghton said, "have you ever been exposed to the poison?"

"—No."

Dr. Houghton looked at the Bishop, then back at Louis. "We are hoping for men who have been through it. They would stand a better chance."

"I have had bouts with malaria. I think I've read that malaria can make a person immune."

Bishop Quintard was a man of unhurried delivery. "Mr. Schuyler, you hardly will find two doctors who agree on anything concerning yellow fever. One says this, the other says that. One prescribes the very thing that the other warns against. All that the medical men know is that they are up against a deadly, deadly enemy."

Louis said, "If God is sovereign, why should I be afraid?"

Neither of his counsellors had an immediate reply.

As he was leaving, they promised him afternoon prayers.

He almost forgot his travelling bag, which he had stationed in a corner of the hall. Turning, fumbling, he got himself in muster. He put on his hat and went through the door with as little awkwardness as possible. His instructions were to talk with Mr. Sword and come back later in the day. Unless an acclimated priest became available, he would be given passes to Memphis.

On Fifth Avenue, where he waited to cross, a carriage pulled over. He received the offer of a ride. He did not recognize the woman at first, but she called him Father Schuyler. She was a refreshing sight, all smiling and fair, her countenance set off by a fashionable hat and the scalloped circle of a dark parasol. He remembered her from somewhere—he remembered her eyes and the lilt of her voice—and then he realized that this was the young widow he had met at Monty's dinner party, the night in the spring.

Louis explained that he was heading for the ferry, that he was on his way to Hoboken. He said the river was far out of her path, surely, and he couldn't think of causing her the inconvenience. But she would hear nothing of the sort. She put a hand to the sun and warned Louis of the heat of the day. In the same breath, and rather lyrically, she told the driver to change course, that they were going to the Hoboken ferry.

Louis yielded to the courtesy and off they started, his travelling bag planted on his lap. They took the corner and soon they were moving at a nice trot. Out of the air, the woman's name came to mind. Winifred Pell, that was it.

Winifred Pell was not in the least dispossessed. "You must tell me of Holy Innocents," she said. "Oh, I keep up with you, Father Schuyler. I see your brother from time to time, and I always inquire about you. I am so happy that you are settled once again, even if it *is* in Hoboken. But then, Holy Innocents is a jewel of a church, from what I hear."

"Yes, the little church is lovely." Now that he had her name handy, Louis was easier.

"And the work is with the poor, I'm told."

"I believe that to be my calling, Mrs. Pell—to work with the poor."

"I might have guessed that of you, Father. I remarked to myself the night we met, this is not a shallow man."

"Come now—"

"What a delightful time that was, that evening at your brother's house. And you played so beautifully. I love a man's touch on the piano. From now on, I shall never hear Handel's *Largo* that I won't think of you."

Louis found that he was unable to deal with the compliment. He said, "George Frederick Handel—now there's a composer."

She said, "People who love music feel a rich kinship with each other, don't you think?"

"Yes—yes, I do," Louis said.

The trot, refined though it was, caused her to sway toward him occasionally.

"I have a piano that is ever silent," she said. "It's very sad, really. But my lack of talent shamed me long ago. I don't suppose that you would like to come by some day when you are in the city and strike a key or two for relaxation, and for an appreciative audience? You would be welcome *any* day. The instrument is terribly out of tune, no doubt, and I shall have it looked after right away, just in case."

"I should like to call," Louis said.

"You are gracious to accept my clumsy invitation. Could I expect you on Saturday?" Her fingers went for a card.

On Saturday, if things turned out, he would be in Memphis.

He told her of his plans. He told her of his visit with Dr. Houghton and Bishop Quintard.

"Father Schuyler," she cried, "why must you be so reckless with yourself?"

He could think of but one answer. "Because of Christ and His Church."

"Forgive me, I am not a very spiritual woman," she confessed. "Have you taken this up with your brother?"

"I thought it best to wait until things are definite. I suspect that he will try to dissuade me even then. Brother knows brother. I'll see him before I leave, of course."

Winifred Pell's effervescence had subsided. Her charm remained a force, nonetheless. She had been like a fountain and now her demeanor was like that of a summer lake reflecting clouds. It would have been a chore for Louis to say which of her moods was the more lifting.

Sitting there beside her as the carriage rumbled and floated along the streets and the avenues, he could taste a spice in the city dust. He seldom had felt this kind of exhilaration—and, deeper, he seldom had felt this kind of melancholy. He knew that if he allowed himself he could be tempted by all the possibilities in life. It was as if the buildings fell away in brightness on either side of the route.

When they reached the ferry landing, she reminded him of the invitation to the piano. "It will be there, tuned, when you come back from your mission."

"Thank you. You are very kind."

Louis stepped down. He noticed that his travelling bag weighed practically nothing.

"God protect you, Father."

"And you, Mrs. Pell." His hat was off.

He lingered to chat politely a minute longer, for the horse took advantage of the stop. They chatted about the blessing that autumn would be. Then the wheels turned again and the parasol danced solemnly at Winifred Pell's shoulder.

·4·

"I SHOULD GO, not you," Mr. Sword said.

"But your absence would be crippling to the parish here," Louis said. "Mine would not. I'm hardly established in my duties."

"I would have no qualms about leaving Holy Innocents in your charge."

"Father Sword, that is a compliment, but—"

"If I could only be certain of God's will."

"Let my going be in your stead. We can think of it that way, can't we?"

"I ask you, are *you* certain of God's will?"

There they stood. They were alone in the common-room. Neither of them had sat down since Louis returned.

"Yes, I think I am."

"Amazing—"

"Is that too much cheek, Father? If it is—"

"No, no, I didn't mean that," Mr. Sword said. "No, I admire your attitude in this. It might even be that I envy. I confess to you, I have had no burning bushes in my life. I am never absolutely certain of the voice of God. Except in scripture, of course."

"I do not claim to have *heard*," Louis said. "Surely you believe that the Lord can speak to us in our bones."

"I do," Mr. Sword conceded. "Come, I'll help you pack."

They went down the corridor, Mr. Sword in the lead.

Mrs. Moffat flitted from here to there, preparing a box of food, ironing collars, ironing handkerchiefs, brushing this and that, doing what she could. "Father Parsons is down," she would moan to herself, blinking at whatever she happened to find in her hands. Then she would collect her faith, visibly, as she worked, and she would hum a snatch of one hymn or another.

"I don't know if this is good or not, your going," she said once, bustling near Louis.

She said it again when he was leaving. "But God bless you in it," she added. She muffled her next words against the coat he wore. "I'll keep you before the Mercy Seat every moment." After that, she hurried her tears toward the back of the clergy-house.

Mr. Sword walked with Louis to the ferry. There was much to say, Louis supposed, but they were silent for the most part. The two-o'clock ferry was approaching the landing, maneuvering, slapping waves. The river threw the broken sun everywhere.

The day seemed three days long already.

A telegram had changed things at Dr. Houghton's. There was a prospect—a possibility, at any rate—of a priest seasoned to the fever. Because of this, the reins were tightened in regard to Louis and the passes.

Shown to Dr. Houghton's study, Louis sat down and gave himself over to a mix of emotions. The respite went against his grain. He did not want to be beguiled by the comfort of feeling protected and safe. The train would leave at six o'clock—he had stopped for a timetable. He still felt that he should be aboard. The arrangements for the new volunteer were not sewn up, might blow into nothing. Louis could not grasp that Dr. Houghton and Bishop Quintard would court further delay.

He sat there for more than an hour, ready, while his counsellors weighed and weighed a decision.

The ferry rocked him to sleep.

A touch on his sleeve awakened him and he was the last passenger to disembark. So here he was, back in Hoboken. He had not expected to see this place again for a time. He was beginning to feel like a pendulum.

It was still Wednesday. It seemed weeks since the morning celebration and the cooler sun at Peekskill, but it was the same day. He switched the box of food to the arm that carried the travelling bag. He dug for his watch and snapped it open. It was a little past six. He thought of the train. As he walked on, though, he was able to put that particular train out of his mind. "Drop back tomorrow," Dr. Houghton had said. "We'll see how things look then." The box of food was an eloquent testimony to the frailty of plans. The food—Louis was sure that it would spoil before this hour tomorrow. He would make it his supper tonight as he had intended, not let Mrs. Moffat's care go to waste.

Rounding a corner, he had to dodge a hoop and then a boy. It was practically a fling for a step or two. The incident rejuvenated him. The sight of Holy Innocents likewise contributed something to his blood. Even in England he had seen no finer "jewel"—save for dimension, of course, and if the surface of the stonework had only had the benefit of all those years.

The next morning, at his request, he went over with Mr. Sword to celebrate the Holy Communion. The eastern light washed the exterior of the church with color. Stone was coming to life. God's creative act went on and on, it seemed, as constant in grace as the Redemption itself.

Louis firmly held with daily celebration. There were those who did and those who didn't. Among those who did were the Sisters of St. Mary, and because of this bond with them, Louis was sensitive to their dependence on the Sacrament. The little band of Sisters in Memphis—how could he not think of them? Without a priest up and around, the offices at the Cathedral must have come to a halt. He saw the Sisters laboring along, cut off from their spiritual refreshment at a time when they most needed the strength and the comfort.

Mr. Sword said to him, "So the night did not change your heart?"

"No, Father. Did you think that it would?"

"I thought there might be a chance. Maybe not your heart, but your mind."

"Perhaps I am too stubborn."

"Perhaps you are. God does ordain circumstances."

Louis did not gather an accusation. The tone was thoughtful, that was all.

In the sacristy, after he had vested and said the Preparations, he turned to Mr. Sword and said, "Let it be our special intention at this celebration that whatever in this matter is of self might come to naught, and whatever is of God might be prospered."

They entered the sanctuary.

The very air hinted of the presence of God. Had Louis been blind, his pores would have detected the distinct weather of this consecrated place. He was not blind and he was glad. Beauty fell all about the morning dimness. And it was more than the windows, Louis thought. *Lord, I have loved the habitation of thy house, and the place where thine honor dwelleth.* The words of David came and were personal.

He believed, theologically, that God could be as real, as close, anywhere—at a reading club, in a music room, on the street, even down a shadowed alley. Christ had said, *Lo, I am with you always.* But Louis had never been able to school his consciousness to this as much as he would have liked. Now, and always at a celebration of the Holy Communion, he sensed that he was moving from that which was abstract toward that which was concrete.

> *Lift up your hearts.*
> *We lift them up unto the Lord.*
> *Let us give thanks unto the Lord our God.*
> *It is meet and right so to do.*
> *It is very meet, right, and our bounden duty, that we should at all times, and at all places, give thanks unto*

thee, O Lord, Holy Father, Almighty, Everlasting God.

Therefore with Angels and Archangels, and with all the company of heaven, we laud and magnify thy glorious Name; evermore praising thee, and saying: Holy, holy, holy, Lord God of hosts, heaven and earth are full of thy glory—

The Body of our Lord Jesus Christ, which was given for thee—

The Blood of our Lord Jesus Christ, which was shed for thee—

Glory be to God on high, and in earth peace, good will towards men. We praise thee, we bless thee, we glorify thee, we give thanks to thee for thy great glory, O Lord God, heavenly King, God the Father Almighty.

O Lord, the only-begotten Son, Jesus Christ; O Lord God, Lamb of God, Son of the Father, that takest away the sins of the world, have mercy upon us—

For thou only art holy; thou only art the Lord; thou only, O Christ, with the Holy Ghost, art most high in the glory of God the Father. Amen.

Mrs. Moffat had prepared the box again. "Well, in the event the Lord opens the way," she said. She let it be known, however, that she wouldn't be unhappy if the box reappeared that evening.

All in all, the departure from the clergy-house seemed more natural than it had the day before.

Mr. Sword walked only the first block. "As a friend, as a mere human," he said to Louis, "I urge you not to take Memphis upon yourself unless you feel there is dire necessity."

·5·

"WE ARE WAITING for a telegram from your father," Dr. Houghton said.

"I don't understand," Louis said, and turned to Bishop Quintard.

The cat came down from the books and left the study.

"Your brother paid us a visit, very upset," the Bishop said, touching his cross.

Winifred Pell, Louis thought. He could not blame her.

"Monty thinks of me as a child," he said.

"My friend," Dr. Houghton said, "it's reasonable that a family would be concerned."

"But I am *not* a child."

The Bishop's fingers lingered at the cross. "Each of us is a child to someone, if we are fortunate."

"It did seem wise," Dr. Houghton said, "to seek your father's consent before allowing you to proceed."

"Then I am under serious consideration?"

"Yes, of course," Bishop Quintard said.

Dr. Houghton was returning to the clutter of money on

his desk. "You are so dedicated, you have persuaded Bishop completely."

"Was the other priest detained?"

"There is a chance that Dr. Dalzell will be able to leave Shreveport in a day or two," Dr. Houghton said.

"We realize there is need for more than one worker," Bishop Quintard said. "So, this is where we stand. Now it is up to your father."

Louis could picture how torn his father must be.

But the answer was on the way, probably, and perhaps by now his father was becoming resigned. His father would not be an obstacle, Louis was sure.

To prove himself useful as he passed the time, he assisted with the counting of the money.

Bishop Quintard had been making appeals to various groups in the city, raising financial help for the sufferers in Memphis, and last night he had spoken to the Medical Society. The doctors had been generous. "Would that they had knowledge to give, as well as money," the Bishop said, posting the figure.

Out in the hall, beside a barrel, the housekeeper and a woman of the parish were sorting through a mountain of bed linens. The Bishop explained to Louis that these items were being collected because a fever death meant that a victim's bedding had to be burned. "With so much going up in smoke, you can imagine the shortage."

When the barrel was packed full, Dr. Houghton nailed the lid on it. He was very precise with the hammer. The housekeeper said, "Father, you should get the sexton to do that," but the Rector went right on with the job, and he seemed rather pleased with his ability.

Louis embraced one side of the barrel, low, and Bishop Quintard the other, at a higher point, and they carried it to the front door, where it would await the express wagon.

"Bishop, you snagged your coat!" the housekeeper wailed, and worked her thumb at the feathering of dark threads.

The other woman let out a trill of despair. "You can't slow these men of God down," she said.

The little stir was interrupted by a Western Union boy.

The arrival of a dispatch always excited Louis. On this occasion the effect was stronger than ever. He wanted to step forward and receive the message into his own hands. He had to fight the impulse.

"For Bishop Charles Quintard," the boy said.

The Bishop read the telegram silently, then aloud. The first words told Louis that this was not the reply from his father. He took in something about a shipment of bourbon for whiskey baths. The plight of Memphis was keeping telegraphers busy all over the country, he supposed.

He haunted the front door the rest of the morning.

Luncheon was informal, around the table in the kitchen, a simple fare of cold herring and cheese and figs. Louis was surprised to find that he was hungry. He usually lost his appetite on the day of a journey.

In the early afternoon he hired a hack and went to the Western Union office. He realized that his appearance there would be to no special avail, that he could not speed the message, yet the Western Union office seemed the right place to do this kind of waiting—and somehow, with strangers, it would be more private.

After inquiring at the counter, he took the end of a

bench and tried to settle down. From the back, every minute or so, came the high and uneven tattoo of Morse code. It was a stimulating clack and Louis was fascinated by its alien music.

Someone had left a disheveled *Times* on the bench. He picked it up and put it in order. He darted from column to column until he came upon an item about Memphis. Eighty-five new deaths were reported.

The door opened. Louis looked up and saw Monty entering. He quickly raised the newspaper and burrowed his face in the print, hoping to conceal himself. He did not want to do battle with his brother. The footsteps went straight to the counter, and he was relieved. He turned slightly, keeping his shield. Monty was sending a message to St. Louis, he figured. It was probably a plea for firmness.

When Monty left, Louis gave him time to walk a block. Then he got up and inquired again. He waited a while longer, in vain, and then went out into the afternoon, exchanging the Morse code for the more resonant throbbing of the city.

It was past four o'clock and the telegram had not arrived at the rectory. The parlor was growing dreary. Louis stood at the window, sat down, stood at the window. He was alone. The train would leave in less than two hours. It was beginning to look as if he would be delayed a second time. Was his father away from home? Yes, he must be out of reach. That was the only explanation that made any sense. Today was Thursday—his clerical responsibilities were lighter. Perhaps he had taken the family to the country, Louis thought. Nobody loved an outing more than his father.

Dr. Houghton came in and stood with him at the window. They stood there in silence, looking out, and when the Rector finally spoke, they continued to look out the window.

"We'll not tie you here. If we do not hear from Dr. Schuyler, it is between you and the Lord."

"Then I shall go."

"I assumed that you would."

"I can have the passes?"

"Yes."

"And your blessing?"

"Yes. There is one thing, however, I want to satisfy in my mind."

"What is that, Father?"

"You are not doing this for merit, are you? I ask because you seem so desperate about the opportunity. If you are doing it for merit, then I refer you to St. Paul. It is of grace, our salvation, not of works. We must stand with our evangelical brethren on that point."

"Merit belongs to Christ," Louis said.

"There you have it," Dr. Houghton said. "Well, that takes care of that." It was as if he had brushed his hands. "My, my—I believe we might enjoy a taste of sherry, now that all this is settled."

"A taste of sherry would be nice," Louis said.

They went to the sideboard in the dining room. Bishop Quintard, who seemed to know of their conversation, joined them there. The cat relinquished the sideboard and left the three to their business. The sherry was much the color of the wood, but with light.

"To the glory of God," the Bishop toasted.

The porter lifted the travelling bag to the net above the seat.

"How much time have we?" Louis asked.

"Be about ten minutes, preacher."

Louis put the box on the seat, then went out and walked farther down the platform, through the gatherings and the steam, to see the iron horse.

"Louis!"

The raised voice came from behind. He turned around and faced his brother.

When their arms came together, Louis could not give himself completely.

Monty was breathing heavily from the pursuit. "I went to Dr. Houghton's. I missed you by a hair. He tells me that Father has not answered. I learned—"

"Yes, Monty, I'm going to Memphis."

"You can't do this. You *must* not."

"I should have come to you. Forgive me. But I knew that there would be a lack of understanding."

"What are you trying to *prove*?"

"I'm sorry, Monty. I'm going to Memphis." Louis freed his sleeve.

"You are trying to prove something. I don't know what it is. You were trying to prove something when you went to England and wanted to make a monk of yourself. You go to such extremes. You are my brother and I can speak frankly. You were not meant for such a fanatical life. Think of your health, Louis. Why can't you settle down and be a *moderate* priest? Look at our father. He has lived a normal, sensible life—and is he not a man of God?"

Louis looked at his brother. "The glory of God *is* a puzzle, isn't it?"

"Don't be so dramatic," Monty said. "The glory of God is not at stake."

"That is true. Your theology is correct."

"Then give this up," Monty said.

"Were you not my blood, I believe I could explain. But there is something quite impossible about the connection."

"Were you not my blood," Monty said, "I wouldn't care a whit. I am thinking of our whole family and how they love you."

The train shuddered.

"I think I should board," Louis said.

"As my father's namesake, I will speak for him. Do not go."

Louis was walking toward the step. He offered his hand to his brother.

Monty would not take the hand until the last minute. Then he clamped it.

There was not a word more.

The train lurched as Louis's foot touched the step. He caught himself and found his way into the car. To the shriek of metal, the journey had begun.

·6·

I⊤ WAS CLOSE to midnight on Friday when the train pulled into Louisville. Tired and feeling misshapen from the hours, Louis stepped down to the gravel. It seemed that the wheels and the rails still vibrated beneath him as he walked toward the station. He had descended at several stops along the trip, to put his feet on the steady earth, to collect something of reality—but all of the stations had kept the motion of the train, had rolled and swayed. Only in Cincinnati had there been time for him to claim his legs. Here in Louisville, on the lantern-lit stream of gravel, he felt that he was walking with a drunken pitch again.

A quiet-faced man in a clerical collar came up to him and said, "You are Mr. Schuyler?"

"Yes," Louis said, after his surprise.

"I greet you in the name of Christ our Lord."

Louis returned the salutation.

"I am Dr. Tschiffely." There was the manner of an

apology. "I have received a dispatch from the dear Bishop Quintard. He wished for me to tell you that your father withholds his consent. I take it that a message arrived after your train left."

Louis turned away and looked at the night. Anger was the one strength he could find. He filled his lungs with it. He was unaccustomed to the emotion, and he discovered that he could almost thrill to its pumping. He was not Louis Schuyler now. In all of his life he had never felt so virile, so muscled. The anger was as much against Bishop Quintard and Dr. Houghton as it was against his father, and as much against this Dr. Tschiffely as anybody.

"I am not a child!"

"I don't know the whole affair, of course," Dr. Tschiffely said. "Perhaps a cup of tea will help. And I have a comfortable room for you. You are to remain with me, if you will, until there is other word."

"I have no mind of my own, do I?"

"As I say, I don't know all of this. Do I understand that you were going to Memphis?"

Louis nodded sharply.

"What a noble idea," Dr. Tschiffely said. "I respect you."

"To be coddled by my father and my family, that is embarrassing enough, but to be coddled by the Church, I find it unbearable." With this burst, much of the bitterness went out of Louis and he realized again how tired he was. He looked at the priest and gave up. He said, "I am under your wing, Father Tschiffely."

"Do you have luggage?"

"My bag," Louis said, somewhat lost.

"I'll speak to the porter."

"Never mind. It's a small bag. I will get it."

Louis slept deeply for a while. But the night turned damp and brought to his bones the memory of his cell, and he went through a string of dreams, all having to do with Cowley St. John. After each dream he would open his eyes and continue to wrestle until he could place himself in the unfamiliar room.

He got up, finally, and closed the window. He went back to the warm dent in the bed and tried to reject the circumstances in which he was caught. Because of the dreams, which had been exaggerations, and for the sake of fairness to Father Benson and the monastery, he applied his thoughts to other aspects of his three months at Oxford—the pleasanter things. There had been the sequence itself—every day had been the same, every day had been dependable in that regard. A life for the glory of God had been straightly defined for him there. He had never had to wonder, "What should I be up to now?" And he had loved the very sameness.

5:30 Rise
5:50 Lauds
6:15 Meditation
7:15 Prime
8:00 The Blessed Sacrament
9:00 Breakfast
9:30 Matins—

Somebody's rooster crowed.

Louis was dressed, his first prayers behind him. He waited. When he heard Dr. Tschiffely padding by the door, he went out and asked for the privilege of celebrating the Holy Communion.

"It would be an honor for our church," Dr. Tschiffely said.

"I don't know that," Louis said, "but thank you. I need a new start."

"I can see that we are kin, you and I," Dr. Tschiffely said.

From the church they went to a small restaurant where Dr. Tschiffely had a table he called his own. "The oats are particularly good here," he informed Louis.

The table was in the back, near the kitchen. The proprietor's wife, a convert of Dr. Tschiffely's, attended them. Before the oatmeal was low in the bowls, she brought a platter of eggs and a toppling mound of thick biscuits, unordered. The attitude of her arms and hands expressed that she was bringing gifts. Louis and Dr. Tschiffely had little time for private conversation, she was so obeisant and so eager to please.

"I still believe my duty is to go to Memphis," Louis said, laying hold upon a pause when she was in the kitchen.

"Something comes to me," Dr. Tschiffely said. "I don't know that it's from God, but I think I should speak."

"Do."

"To live might be the higher calling. Have you considered that?"

"You are assuming that I would die of the fever?"

"If you were to go to Memphis, there would be the likelihood. Why should we mince words? We are Christians. Christians can afford to take a more realistic view than anyone else, I daresay."

"I believe that God would protect me," Louis said.

Dr. Tschiffely buttered a biscuit. "Bluntness is not my nature, but I shall be blunt." He looked up at Louis as though for an invitation. He did not wait, however. He said, "I don't think that one should be enamoured of dying in the line of Christian duty."

Louis resented the remark. He wondered if the priest thought of him as some sort of unbalanced opportunist, some ardent young plunderer ready to grab Heaven. At best, it made him feel that he was deemed an oddity, a young man who meant *too* well, who perhaps was unhandy with this earthly life. A reply would only serve to carry the matter further, he thought, and he went on with his breakfast, chewing thoughtfully, hoping his expression was agreeable. A fresh pock on his cheek could not have made him more conscious of his face. He was relieved when the woman came back within earshot.

The conversation turned to the goodness of the coffee.

When the woman took leave the next time, Dr. Tschiffely got to his point again. It seemed of utmost importance to him that Louis find truth in what he was saying. "Perhaps the hardest test of devotion to God is a *life*. It is not always easy, this business of *living* for the glory of God. Perhaps in the long course this is the finer sacrifice."

Louis was listening. With a separate mind, he was composing the telegram he would send to the Sisters in Memphis. Dr. Tschiffely was saying nothing to which he could take exception.

Louis narrowed the message down to this: *I am in Louisville awaiting orders. May I come?*

To his father he wrote: *If there be need, I feel assured that I am only doing my duty. It will be very painful to act in opposition to your command, and nothing but the conviction that I must obey God would cause me to do it. I think I am only receiving the words of the Lord Jesus, "Whosoever loveth father or mother more than me is not worthy of me."*

An answer from Memphis came that afternoon, from Sister Hughetta. An evasive answer, it still touched on things directly. *The Sister Superior and Sister Thecla are hopelessly ill. The Reverend Charles Parsons is dying. We have no priest.*

A telegram from New York, from Bishop Quintard to Dr. Tschiffely, arrived before night. *We have learned that Mr. Parsons is dead. Let Mr. Schuyler go on.*

And so it was settled once more.

Louis thought of Mrs. Moffat in Hoboken. He barely knew her, but he didn't know Mr. Parsons at all, except through connections in Christ, and it was Mrs. Moffat that he saw when the death of Mr. Parsons swept over him. Her visage made the death imaginable.

Even as he thanked God for restoring his manhood, he began to know that courage could be as dark as fear.

·7·

THE TRAIN he boarded at midnight was a combination of passenger coaches and baggage coaches. The conductor would not allow him ignorance of the fact that the baggage coaches were full of coffins for Memphis.

The town of Louisville, motionless, slipped off into the past. It was a perfect night for a train, if one could think now of travel for the sake of travel. A lighted sky traced the hills and brought out the fields flowing by. The occasional whistle told Louis of all the farewells he had ever known. In the sound was also the cry of adventure, and it was strange that it should help, for Louis saw himself as the sort of man who would be staunchly contented with his hearth, had he one of his own. But deep in every man, he supposed, was the notion that it was better to be on a train than not. When the whistle blew and the call stretched thin across the night, one had to believe that any journey could be sweet to the soul.

He was able to doze now and then.

A woman sat alone on the other side of the aisle. She sat

with her back slightly toward her window, her cheek resting against a small pillow, her hair loosened and falling about. Certain improprieties were unavoidable on a train coach. To Louis, there was something luxurious about the freedom of it all, despite the lack of comfort. The woman was sleeping soundly, or so it seemed. Shadows veiled her face. But she was young, there was no doubt about that, and she was company over there—flesh and spirit. He could almost find a coziness when he closed his eyes in appreciation of this stranger who rode through the night with him.

Where was she going? Surely she wasn't going to Memphis, he thought. Perhaps she would get off at some little station down the way, maybe a plantation stop, before the train reached the thick of the pestilence. He prayed so. Yes, he could see her returning to her family at this time, to be near them in their fright. It might be that she was returning with hopes of persuading them to flee before the poison got that far. He pictured her mother a widow, given to swooning, helpless to make a decision. There were no sons, and this was the eldest daughter. She was needed. His speculation included a Cincinnati husband—a giant of a man, and older—who had forbidden her to make this dangerous trip. What a scene that must have been. How understandable the disagreement was, from both viewpoints. Louis preferred not to play it out in his mind. God help her, he thought. She is as headstrong as I am.

They sat near the back. Their fellow-passengers were situated forward, beyond empty seats. Phantom heads swayed toward the aisle, swayed toward the windows. At times, from the front, a woman's voice carried through the coach. The words dropped off somewhere, but the tone came all the way. Louis could have put together a life for that person as well. He chose not to, though. He had picked the right seat and he was thankful.

Before morning, the earth disappeared and rain bled at the window. The new weather pulled him back into his own life, into his own future. He tried to study the flooding patterns on the glass. There was no chance of following a single drop as it was driven along. The rivers from the impact were too many, the currents were too strong. A stream would break apart and shoot to other streams. When he thought about it, he was convinced the glory of God was involved even in those paths. Yet he wondered if he pushed his theology too far. He had to admit that he felt hollow and lonely, no matter how sure his calling, no matter how personal his Christ.

Dawn was practically a secret. The coach kept most of the shadows of the night. In time, however, there was a stirring and a straightening across the aisle. He got out his Prayer Book when there was light enough to read. He hoped he did not make too prim a silhouette.

It was into the morning.

Here came the woman from the front, the one whose voice had surfaced again and again. Her red hair seemed to be throwing her hat off its perch. She was making her way toward the rear of the coach, pausing to get acquainted wherever a seat was occupied by a member of her own sex. And she was not exactly slighting the men, Louis noticed. Her babble ran first in one direction and then in another.

The rain had stopped, but without a promise of the sun. The whole sky was a cloud. The day was growing warm and heavy. Louis grappled with his window and opened it. His coat was as damp as if the window had been open all along. The train was rounding a bend, with the engine visible as it plowed on, and the smoke barreled down and charged at the coaches, and flew above, gray against gray. Soot gathered in his mouth. He knew how his collar must look.

The red-haired woman had tied up next to the passenger opposite him. "Well then, we have something in common," she was saying to her. "We nurses need to keep our shoulders together. Where do you hail from?"

Louis did not catch the answer. But if the young woman by the window was a nurse, his fabrication had already proven to be in vain. She was going to Memphis, evidently, and there was nothing that he could do about it.

With precision, the older nurse got down to a fresh telling of the tales. It was as if she had produced needle and thread. She had heard, she had heard, she had heard. The frenzy at the Memphis depot when the first cases of the fever were reported—it was all too vivid in her second-hand narrative. Louis might as well have been there on the platform himself, shoved to and fro, the coaches packed to the doors and spilling over. "The rudeness! I hear that men and boys opened the windows from the outside and climbed in on top of poor suffocating ladies. I reckon there will always be animals." She devoted a time to the houses which stood unattended while families camped in the woods out from the town. "But a mind doesn't like to stay on *that,* of course," she said. "—At any rate, I finally realized I couldn't sit by when I was needed. I spent a summer in Memphis once, back before the war. I'm hoping my acquaintances got away. I can't figure why *everybody* didn't up and leave. Then there's the other side—most of them who did met shotgun quarantines everywhere they went. Think of those people on the steamers—up and down the river looking for a landing that wouldn't shoo them off. Oh, it's hard to find a Christian these days. Did you hear about the Golden Crown? The fever broke out on board and they say the people would wave for help when the other boats came along, but the other boats steamed right on by them. They were stranded!"

This was the Lord's day. Louis had almost forgotten.

Once, in the middle of the afternoon, taking the air at a country station, he managed an opportunity to face the younger nurse straight on. Passing on the platform, they acknowledged each other's presence. Her eyes came at him like a child's, without blinking, and he had to glance away. Her chin—after she was gone, in that next moment—appeared as breakable as fine china. He looked out at a pasture where two horses bobbed and turned, frolicsome as butterflies, and where a settled oak seemed to be waiting for the last trumpet.

The train was slowing again. Crossings were more frequent now. Ahead, a neighborhood was taking shape. Off to the left, in the distance, a steeple met a flash of late sun. The streets were fringed with a thin, ragged snow. In

September? "Lime for disinfecting," the conductor explained, on sea legs, moving forward through the coach. Houses began to pass, tight in their yards, a steady row, and every house wore a shut look. Memphis gave the impression that it was sleeping the afternoon away.

Then a woman bolted from a house and ran for the gate at the walk, her arms spread wide at first, as if she had an embrace to give, and then she was snatching at her gown and sinking as she ran. Louis pulled into the window and tried to hold on to the scene. The woman was down, like a sheet blown from a clothesline. She had fallen shy of the fence and was blurred by the cadence of the iron pickets. Soon she was lost behind the hedge that bordered the next yard.

Louis let his gaze fall upon the stretch beside the tracks. He saw a mattress docked against a stand of weeds. A gentle smoke peeled from the mattress and crawled along the weeds, hardly lifting. He wondered how many children had come forth on that mattress, and how many deaths had honored it before this last death. It seemed to Louis that a mattress was too intimate a thing to be thrown to the open world. His childhood filled him as he remembered the secret smell of his parents' bed airing in a room where curtains waved with spring. He closed his eyes. A different rhythm caused him to open them. The train was rumbling across a trestle. Below, on a creek bank powdered white, another mattress burned, and the smoke might have been a little fog drifting low over the yellow water. The span lasted but a moment. Willows went by.

At the sound of the whistle, places of business rolled into view. Not a front showed life. A series of clanks and jolts brought the train down to a chug. The conductor entered the coach. "Memphis!" He sounded as if he were announcing an ordinary destination, but under his breath he added, "God help us," and looked straight at Louis.

The directness of the man's eyes made Louis shift, and for the first time since he had read the telegram at Peekskill, he felt a question about what he should do.

But it was too late to doubt, too late to listen to the arguments. He was here.

It was incredible.

How had it happened?

Why had nobody stopped him?

·PART TWO·

·8·

THERE WERE NO HACKS at the depot. The travellers were scattering on foot, seeing to their own encumbrances. Louis offered service to his unnamed companion, but she smiled a refusal. Her valise was small. She had taken up with the red-haired woman, who appeared to know what was what and where to lead her. The lime, like a genuine snow, deepened the hush of the town. Here and there the white trails were sullied by wheel tracks, but not a carriage of any kind could be seen.

After an indecisive start, Louis went back to the depot and asked for directions. He and the agent had the place to themselves now. The agent was confused for a moment about *which* St. Mary's. Louis explained that he was seeking St. Mary's, Episcopal. He waited while the agent thought.

"Two blocks up, turn left," the agent said, pointing, "then bear to the right when you come to the fork. That will be Alabama Street. It will take you out to Poplar, smack at it. The crow couldn't do much better."

Louis set out again, bag in hand.

He passed the black camel-humps of a coal yard, then a deserted livery stable, then one boarding house after another. The rocking chairs on the porches faced each other stiffly. Occasionally there was a straggle of old, beaten petunias, and the smell of them drifted with the smell of smoke and ashes. A naked boy with a moon belly and a button of a penis stood in front of a pinched-looking house, a violated cherub, squalling. Louis went to the child and knelt in the grass.

"Hello there," Louis said. He wanted to help, and he didn't know what to say. He reached out.

Quick as a monkey, the child was up the stone at the door and through the ramshackle frame.

Louis rose and brushed at his knees. Venturing forward, he called to the unseen in the house, "Is there something I can do?"

There was only the crying of the child.

Forcing himself, he stepped inside. The stench choked him. He stepped carefully over an offensive little island on the floor and made his way farther into the tilted house, toward the door in the next room. He stopped. Two bony legs extending from a tangle of cover—that was all he saw. The legs appeared to belong to a woman, but he could not tell for sure. Out of sight, near the head of the bed, the child was still crying.

"I am here to be of help," Louis called, rooted to the spot. He felt weak and totally unarmed for any answer that might come.

There was no answer.

The legs on the bed might have been marble.

And so might his have been, for he was powerless to advance.

He lifted his hands. "Peace be to this house, and to all that dwell in it," he said, and went for the daylight.

He retrieved his travelling bag from the grass and walked up the middle of the street, his sense of mission frustrated. He wondered at his failure. Why had his boldness collapsed? Why had he not entered that other room? *Someone* was needed there, no matter how indelicate the intrusion. A weight came down upon him, although he asked himself what he possibly could have done.

The story of the town grew more explicit as he went along. Charred bedding lay in the gutters. There was hardly a block without a smudge somewhere along the side. And there were the scraps that had escaped, that lay where they had flown—wads of cotton stuffing, loose feathers, the scorched rag of a sheet, the surviving diamonds of a patchwork quilt. He saw a furniture wagon stacked with coffins. Black coffins rode with raw pine boxes and lost some of their richness and formality by the association.

Farther on was a bridge that forded a white-edged carpet of slime. Beyond it, he found the fork. He bore to the right. A buggy came along, rattling across the bridge behind him. It turned for Alabama Street too, and slowed down as it overtook him.

"I suggest you save your strength," the man said. He placed an authoritative hand on the empty seat at his side, then gave the hand back to the reins.

Louis accepted gratefully.

And he remembered at that instant another scene.

But how far he was from Fifth Avenue now, and from Winifred Pell and the innocence of the ride which she had offered him. He wished for a magic to return him to Wednesday. *Never.* God was a worker of miracles, not a worker of magic. Courage came back to him when he reminded himself of that. He sat erect as the buggy started off. He couldn't believe he had not entered the room where the two legs lay like marble.

He introduced himself and told where he was going. "I've just arrived in Memphis. I'm from a church in Hoboken."

"New Jersey? That's a far piece."

"Indeed it is."

It turned out that the man was a doctor. His report of conditions was simply that he could not remember when he had put his head down. He sent Louis a look. "You better go back North," he said, "or you'll get whipped with the rest of us."

There was a loud punctuation to the warning. It was not thunder—there was no roll to it. There was the one sharp clap, very close, and the ghost of it in the silence that followed. Louis learned from the doctor that a cannon was fired every hour, that some of the desperate experts believed the poisonous spores might be dissipated in that way. It was obvious, from the doctor's face, that he didn't see much hope in the tactic. The thought struck Louis, however, that the battle against the fever was ennobled and somehow clarified by the sound of actual war.

Trees crowded the neighborhood. Most of them were old-timers. Thick with green in the lingering summer, they stood protectively about the yards. The houses—some were stately and some were not—achieved a formidable reserve. Louis was intensely conscious of doors and windows, house after house, but he was hesitant to pry and he took only glances. The street had a gentle rise. At a point on the right, up ahead, a church roof emerged.

"There you are, Reverend, my boy," the doctor said. "St. Mary's. Do me a favor, young man. Why do they call it a Cathedral?"

Louis was pleased to oblige. "Because it's the Bishop's church. He has a chair there. Bishop Quintard, of the Diocese of Tennessee."

"That so? I've never been inside the place. I'm a Baptist, myself."

Little by little, the boards and battens cleared beneath the ecclesiastical pitch of the roof. A wooden cathedral was no less a Cathedral, Louis told himself. The steeple lagged. It was at the far end, coming from behind a screen of leaves. It was the one he had glimpsed from the train.

He was vaguely disappointed to find that they were approaching the rear. The Cathedral faced the thoroughfare toward which Alabama Street was heading at an angle, and from here it materialized not as a structure of especial beauty. He was eager for the entrance. He had pictured himself receiving the welcome of the doors a long way off. He had known church doors to reach out, even when closed. A pull like that would have been fitting for the last mile of his journey. But he supposed the thought was grandiose, and worse than that, selfish. *To the glory of the Reverend Mr. Schuyler,* he realized, pained.

The street came sharply to the intersection, at such a cut that the grounds took the shape of a pie-wedge. Then the horse was geeing toward the front of the Cathedral. Louis could see the low-gabled narthex. By the time the buggy came to a halt, his feet were over the side.

·9·

HE WENT IN.

The sunlight there was like a thin smear of butter. Wooden arches framed the darkness aloft. St. Mary's did not speak to him in quite the way that Holy Innocents did, it was true, but the restraint was appealing. Symmetry and peace were broken only by his own presence. Nobody else was there.

His knee and his travelling bag touched the aisle, beside the back pew. He did his praying quickly and went out to the business at hand.

A Sister of St. Mary happened along. "Mr. Schuyler? Our Lord is good to us. You have come. I was this minute returning from a call." Her tongue was native to the region—the soft, drowsy syllables floated as on a song. "I am Sister Hughetta. It was I who answered your telegram."

"Father" was not used by every member of the communion, and so far as Louis was concerned, "Mr. Schuyler" did just as well. He wished he would not even notice. "How are the Sisters?" he asked.

"Sister Constance, our Sister Superior, is very low. It is only a matter of time, I'm afraid. And Sister Thecla is also failing. The rest of us—" Her voice trailed off without a definite report.

"I should like to see Sister Constance and Sister Thecla, as soon as I'm put away."

"I think it not best, Mr. Schuyler. Not today." The wimple accentuated her classical face and came close to hiding the weariness etched on her brow. "It is late. These are the hours that can be so trying. The patients must be kept as unexcited as possible."

"—I understand."

"Don't fret. Dr. Dalzell is planning to look in this evening."

"The priest from Shreveport? He has arrived already?"

"Yesterday."

"Oh."

Louis forced his mind to a rightful appreciation. It wasn't as if he had lost a race or anything like that, he told himself.

"Perhaps," Sister Hughetta said, "I should have urged you not to come, but there was no way to tell how long we would be without."

"Not a bit of it," Louis said. "I wanted to be here."

"This morning we were able to resume our practice of daily celebration, and you know how precious that is to us. Yes, he took the Cup to them. Our Lord provided a lovely rose for the tray. In the midst of all this."

"Think of that," he said.

"And blessing on top of blessing, Dr. Dalzell is a man of medicine."

Louis made an effort to reflect her wonder. "So I was told," he said, and tried not to think of himself as less than a soldier.

Sister Hughetta cradled an empty basket in one arm. Her free hand behaved formally as she introduced the buildings that flanked the Cathedral. In the narrowed yard on the corner stood the school and sister-house, which somehow seemed poised for flight, and in the other yard, on the town side, stood the Bishop's house, the house where Dean Harris lay with the fever.

"Does the Dean know that you've arrived?" she asked.

"Not as yet," Louis said.

Plainly, Sister Hughetta was not inviting him into the sister-house.

"And who are you again?" the Dean asked. His sallow fingers dragged at his beard.

Louis had been talking with him for five minutes or more. "My name is Louis Schuyler," he said, taking a step closer to the bed.

"Of course—Dr. Schuyler's boy." The carding of the beard was futile. "Somebody mentioned that we were looking for you."

"They tell me that you are improving," Louis said. "I am thankful to hear it."

"I still wander."

"It will take time, naturally."

"We lost Mr. Parsons," the Dean said. "He died in this

house, in the next room. One man is taken, one man is spared. The mind of the Almighty is beyond us. Did you know Parsons?"

"I regret to say that I didn't."

"Charlie Parsons was a true servant."

Louis affirmed as much with silence. Then he said, "I am presently assisting at Holy Innocents, in Hoboken, and the people there remembered him and loved him."

"Gone. Swept away. It seems such a tragedy."

"—From this side."

"This is the only side I'm really familiar with," the Dean said tiredly.

It sounded as though a doubt or two might have stolen into the weakened body and lodged somewhere within the skull. It was the way he said it, more than the simple statement, that disturbed Louis. Honesty was never a sin—and what Dean Harris had muttered was certainly a fact, physically—but where was the faith? The voice, by its downwardness, might have belonged to a skeptic. Here was the priest of the Cathedral, a man with godly responsibilities. His remark was as depressing as the mussed bed-sheets and the air in the room. Was it possible that the fever could ravage so deeply? Could faith itself fall victim? Louis longed for a cleaner twilight, for a breath that would not taste stale. There were spores of one kind and spores of another kind, he thought. There were diseases of the body and diseases of the spirit. Given this room for flowering, might one contagion be as virulent as the other? He must hold out against the smallest seed of disbelief.

He said, "Our duty, as I understand it, is to worship and

to serve, and not to try to fathom God's purposes."

"Well put," the Dean said. "But how young you are to have reached that."

Something in the tribute made Louis flinch. He said, "For the work here, Father, I believe that my years, or my lack of them, will be in my favor."

"I hope so. I think of poor old Dr. White from Calvary Church. Last I heard, he was going out to the cemetery early every morning and staying the day long. They claim that as soon as he finishes one service another funeral meets him at the gate. His activity might have ceased by now, of course. Have you learned whether or not he's still with us?"

"No, Father, I've only arrived. I shall inquire. Perhaps you would want me to take his duties."

"Oh, but the living need us."

"Tell me what to do and I will do it."

"I am here, my young brother, but I am out of all this. Do whatever Dr. Dalzell tells you. I've turned the helm over to him. He's a capable man and I thank God for sending him."

"I look forward to meeting Dr. Dalzell," Louis said.

Dark was near.

Louis lighted the lamp. He left the room soon afterwards, for he could sense that Dean Harris had exhausted himself.

Mrs. Bullock apologized for the supper she set before him. She explained that the markets were closed and rations were running low. "And they warn us, don't eat this, don't eat that," she said. "Maybe it's good that we have to get by on as little as possible. Maybe it helps to save us."

"This is fine for me," Louis said, and he told the woman that he admired her for staying on and putting her own safety at naught.

"The Sisters are my family," she said quickly. "I could never leave them."

"God will honor your loyalty."

"That has nothing to do with it."

The woman was not gentleness all the way through.

Tonight, unsure of his actual mettle, Louis felt needy of such a spirit in himself. Infect me with *this,* he thought. He absorbed as much of her as he could. The savor of that fierce, steadfast love braced him and more than made amends for the dull broth. The presence of Christ in her became a palpable doctrine for him while he sat there— became as blessed a mystery, and as fortifying, as the presence of Christ in the Sacrament.

His attention followed Mrs. Bullock's eyes to the hall door when footsteps whispered down the stairs.

A distraught nun entered the room. Without addressing Louis, she asked Mrs. Bullock to heat water for a mustard footbath, and informed her that Sister Hughetta had taken the headache now and was fainting away. Then the herald of the upsetting news turned to him. He had risen. She introduced herself as Sister Ruth, uttered a welcome, and giving not a moment after courtesy was done, swept to the hall and up the stairs.

Mrs. Bullock was off to the kitchen.

Louis tagged along, desiring to be of assistance.

There was little to do but stoke the embers and pour the

water from the bucket to the kettle, and Mrs. Bullock was very fast.

"One by one," she said. "Sister Constance, Sister Thecla, now Sister Hughetta. I should have suspected. Sister didn't seem herself when she came in from the call."

"I talked with her when I arrived," Louis said. "It was only two hours ago. I could tell that she was worn, but I never had an inkling."

"Mr. Schuyler—that's how it is with anything, isn't it? From one hour to the next, we never know what the Lord will send."

"You're quite right."

"The difference is, well, that under these conditions we can make a fairly good guess."

"I commend you for speaking about it so serenely."

"I do have a question, if I let myself think. *Is* it God that sends the yellow jack?"

On the stove-top, a bead of water sizzled.

Louis fought for a safe answer to give the woman. Until this point in his ministry he had managed to remain innocent of private conjecture in dealing with strenuous doctrines, and, God helping him, he would uphold the teachings of the Church and not resort to expounding fugitive notions now. He referred her to the beginning of the prayer that implied the acceptable understanding: *O Almighty God, who in thy wrath didst send a plague upon thine own people in the wilderness*—*and, also in the time of King David, didst slay with the plague of pestilence threescore and ten thousand, and yet remembering thy mercy didst save the rest*—

He was instructing a sure believer and he saw no

dismay. Her look of faith did not stumble in the least. He could imagine the calculated arguments that some of the more severe thinkers might employ to chip at the whole idea of a merciful God at a time like the present. If he looked into his own mind far enough, he could understand the attitudes that some people might take. The glory of God did indeed have a dark side. Or, from one perspective it was so torturously bright it caused total blindness. For the sake of orthodoxy, that was the better way to express the problem. The Epistle of James had God as the Father of lights, with whom there was no variableness, neither shadow of turning. He would not want to subtract from the magnificence of that thought.

The heat in the kitchen grew burdensome. Before the kettle went into sounds of eruption, Mrs. Bullock lifted it.

Louis frowned. "A hot footbath on a night like this, and the person feverish. It seems almost cruel, doesn't it?"

"To bring the perspiration. It's very important, the first thing to do if the patient is dry and burning."

"Here, let me," he offered.

At last he was doing something, and yet how minor it was.

Mrs. Bullock climbed the stairs with him. She took over again when they reached Sister Hughetta's room, and immediately she and Sister Ruth converged upon the figure dropped in the chair. Louis was willing to withdraw and leave matters in their charge. The pan was in place. He closed the door, but the sighs of the patient and the entreaties of the attendants could still be heard as he explored to another room.

A Sister, a face from somewhere else, came forward to greet him. "We met once at the house in New York," she said.

"That we did," Louis said, pleased that she recollected. "But your name—I have no excuse—"

"I am Sister Clare. How kind you are, Father Schuyler, to have come here to help us. What a brave heart you must have. I'm not easy about you, though. We have heard that you are not acclimated."

"I lean on God," was all he could say.

"Nevertheless, be careful of the night air. It is most treacherous."

The bed dominated the room. The flattened occupant was asking, "Who is there?"

Sister Clare returned to her post beside the bed. "My Sister, Father Schuyler is with us now. Father, our Sister Superior."

A hand, as if remembering its youth and health, roused from the bed-sheet. Louis moved in and took the fingers into his. The flame in the room was low and Sister Constance seemed to miss when she looked up for him. At the same time, but not at all because of the poor light, he was unable to find the Sister Constance he had met on several occasions. Why, she had been no more than thirty-five, if that. They were not really meeting again, he realized.

"O Lord, open thou our lips," he said.

"And our mouth shall shew forth thy praise." Sister Constance was remarkably clear with the words.

"O Lord, make speed to save us," he said.

"O Lord, make haste to help us."

Never had the versicle and response been more apropos, he thought.

Recalling that Sister Hughetta had questioned the wisdom of his being here during these hours, he cut his visit short. He was on his way to the stairs when, from a door down the hall, there burst toward him a nun bent on escape, delirious, and behind her came another nun, gaining on her, fetching her. "*Thecla, Thecla*—you *must* be quiet. Come back to bed now. Be a dear."

So that was Sister Thecla.

She cried, "I see the Lord!"

"No, Sister," her captor said, "that is only the young priest from the North."

Louis went on to the stairs and down, to remove his part of the disorder. He went outside and sat on the step. Sister Thecla's mistake had jarred him. His feeling of inadequacy, which had camped in the back of his mind ever since his walk from the station, now came on in full assault as he gazed at the dark above the houses across the street. He could not help asking himself if perhaps in Peekskill he had made a mistake of the same magnitude as Sister Thecla's a moment ago. She had seen the Lord, but it wasn't the Lord. He had felt the Lord's hand upon him, but had he really? And if not, what had caused *his* delirium?

It appalled him to think that he might have obeyed a mere impulse. Could the prompting have been a sudden appetite for adventure? A passion to be a hero? A misguided desire to plunge into the suffering of Christ? He would have to stop thinking about it or he would have one of his spells. He believed he had earnestly committed himself to God for His purpose, whatever that meant, and he must cling to that as the only reason for his being here. But even so, he wondered if he would have come if he had once paused long enough to really consider the prospects.

The moon was in the trees—a lover's moon, Louis thought. There was no mercy in its charm, and he found himself drawn to the church door, like a mouse to a mouse-hole.

The questions would not stop. Keeping to prayer was almost impossible. He was trying to offer himself afresh, and yet he was wondering if he had a choice now, and wondering if his retreat to God's house was purely for cloistral peace. It occurred to him that his gravitation to this interior tonight was perhaps a sign of weakness. He was glad of the verse—what was it?—about the Lord's strength being made perfect in weakness. Although the wood of the kneeler was not necessarily the means of that particular grace, he liked to attend God in as literal a fashion as he could, so that his flesh imitated what he pictured of his spirit. If he couldn't completely control his mind, he could at least control his body.

But not always. He had not been able to command himself physically into the bedroom of that little house on the way from the train. He had followed the boy, that miniature of crying humanity, to a point—he had been able to go so far but no farther. Was that halted act to be symbolic of his larger mission? What precisely was he to *do* in this city of death? It was all very murky in his mind. He had no knowledge of remedies or doctoring. Dr. Dalzell from Louisiana was the prepared man. As for the continuance of daily celebration, Dr. Dalzell could handle that too—*was* handling it.

I have disregarded my father, he thought. I know him. He is surely in pieces now. All for nothing, all for this muddle.

Mental havoc could never amount to prayer—or could it? Louis, who believed in disciplined worship and supplication, who at times in the past had almost found the "prayer of silence" within his range, hoped that the Holy Spirit would take these extemporal concerns, these blunderings of despair, and make of them one acceptable plea. Even that was selfish, he supposed. Yet Christ had said, "Ask and ye shall receive."

His eyes were open to the gloom of the sanctuary. The stained moonlight died inside the lancets. The altar and the fine work of the reredos he had to accept by faith. If only he could concentrate on the glory of God without trying to *solve* it, he thought.

Into the silence came a faint rumble and squeak, a buggy in the night. The distance shrank and the gait of the horse broke up on the approach.

Louis slipped out of the pew. He went to the door and opened it a crack. The moonlight seemed to confirm that here was the volunteer he had heard about, the man under whom he would serve. Stepping down from the buggy was a lone priest with a doctor's satchel.

Hesitation was not in order.

Louis hurried forth. "Am I addressing Dr. Dalzell?" he asked.

"Yes, my dear young brother, and who are you?" The priest, the hitching done, extended his hand.

"Louis Schuyler. From Hoboken, New Jersey. I have come to render such assistance as I can in this dreadful time. The Dean says to see you and do what you say."

"Are you related to my friend, Dr. Schuyler of St. Louis?"

"He is my father. I am glad to know that you and he are friends. It will comfort him to know that I am here with you."

"Have you experience with yellow jack?"

"Not really."

"You mean you've never been exposed?"

"Not until this afternoon."

"I'm shocked that you've come. Do you realize the risk you are running?"

"Fully," Louis said. He was trembling some.

"Please excuse my saying so," Dr. Dalzell said, "but you are a fool."

Louis swallowed. "I am here for Christ and the Church. Do not call me that, I beg. Whatever happens is God's will."

Dr. Dalzell softened then and hooked arms warmly with Louis as they walked toward the sister-house. "Well, where would the world be without fools? Where would *God* be? But you do seem a nervous sort, hardly suited for the duty here."

"That isn't fair," Louis protested. He hoped that his words were not shrill. "What you see is my eagerness to get to work. I am ready to begin tonight."

"Out of the question, fatigued as you are. Your long journey is written all over you. Get a refreshing sleep and be ready for the morning. I think it advisable that you take quarters with me at the Peabody Hotel. It's about the only place—"

"Couldn't I put up at the Dean's?"

"Mr. Parson's room can't be used. Death provides no vacancy. That's a rule to which I stick. Precaution is the word. The other two beds are occupied. The Dean has an old friend, Major Somebody-or-other, confined in one of them."

"But I had hoped—you see, Father, I would very much like to remain near the Cathedral." Whether this desire was spiritual or fleshly, Louis had no idea.

"I'm not much for it," Dr. Dalzell said, "but perhaps we could throw a pallet in the Dean's parlor."

·10·

LOUIS FELL ASLEEP before the floor defeated his back.

He awoke at dawn, with an ache that ran the length of him. Resurrection was a labor. Had Dr. Dalzell not given him charge of an early Eucharist, he would have dropped to the blankets again, regardless of the hard base. The morning into which he was moving had a rigidity of its own.

He performed his toilet in foreign rooms off the hall, searching around, timidly. He felt like an unsuccessful thief in this attempt to prepare himself for the day. Something about his reflection appeared unsound, and it wasn't the fault of the vague glass. Not until he stood at the altar did he achieve a sense of being hale and furnished. It was strange, he thought, that a man would find his surest current in the spot where he felt the least worthy.

The assemblage at the rail was like a depleted, linear army. There were but five mouths, and his own, for Bread and Wine. First in the row was Sister Ruth, her thanksgiving strained but recognizable. Next was Sister Clare, who wore her composure as a bride would wear white. Then there was Sister Frances, who simply looked hungry. "She tends the orphan asylum down the road," Sister Clare had informed him. Shoulder to shoulder the sisters knelt, and then there was a young woman with expectant eyes, a communicant from the neighborhood, suitably hatted, whose dress was soiled but showed taste and wherewithal. Down further was Mrs. Bullock, and her placed hands told more of her life than her lips ever would. Behind the kneeling figures, the nave yawned emptily.

And yet, no matter now spare this guard, Louis was confident that the "cloud of witnesses" compassed about, joining them in praise, and joining them in their human concerns as well. He suspected, as did all of his close allies, that the veil between the Church Triumphant and the Church Militant was at its thinnest whenever the Holy Communion was celebrated. *They are in Christ, we are in Christ, Christ is here.* No doubt the mystery was just as substantial every minute of every day, but a mortal was most sensitive to it in the Sacrament. What a benefit, this *tangible* grace. And how encouraging it was to detect those spirits who enjoyed its essence continually. They seemed as real to him as the Dean and the Sisters who lay waiting in their rooms. Why shouldn't they? They were healthier by far.

Sister Clare accompanied Louis on the rounds to the infirm ones. He stopped initially at the bedside of Dean Harris. The Dean claimed to be improved—but, except for the almost vulgar smack when he received the Sacrament, he appeared as robbed of vitality as he had the night before. On the Dean's instructions, Louis took the elements to the guest in the house, Major Mickle, who was very appreciative and very confused. Then he went to Sister Constance. She had lasted the night—that was about all that could be said. Her responses were far away now. The situation in Sister Hughetta's room turned awkward and beyond help, with vomit preventing the Sacrament. Dealing with Sister Thecla was impossible too, for she was swatting at a dream of bats around her bed and would not be stilled.

After administering to the nuns who had stayed behind to attend the patients, he went back to the Cathedral and completed the duties there. Dr. Dalzell's absence was understandable. The entire city was in need. Louis persuaded himself that things had been done as "decently and in order" as possible.

The young woman of the neighborhood waylaid him between the church and the Dean's residence. She was worried about her father. That he was down with the fever was only incidental, she seemed to imply.

"My father is an infidel," she said.

While they talked, they began to catch a rain.

It might have been a library instead of a bedroom. But the books did not look interesting to Louis. They were *too* neatly regimented, for one thing, and the nearby titles indicated nothing that would stir his heart. There was law and more law, and economics, and science. No poetry, no novels, no histories, no biographies. The dearth of philosophy expressed a certain mind. Even if he hadn't been told, Louis thought he would have guessed the sort of man he was visiting now. Still, because the spines gave off the subtle warmth of volumes that have been held and read, he sensed at least a small compatibility with this person. It was like finding a vein through which a river could flow. That was good. He doubted if God would ever be conveyed by an indifferent or forced witness.

He tried to keep a quiet tone. "How can you curse God if He doesn't exist?" he said, mopping along Mr. Alberson's neck and chest with a sponge of iced whiskey.

"It's only a figure of speech," the man said, shuddering. "Please—leave me in peace. This business of dying is all I can handle at the moment. Let me be on with it."

"The peace which Christ won for us on the Cross—that's the peace I wish for you, Mr. Alberson."

"I have no quarrel with you Christians and your teachings. But the story is not for me. God so loved the world—isn't that how it reads? I have no time for such romance."

They were alone in the room. Louis dipped the sponge again and brought it forth, wrung, fresh with the whiskey. The man looked patriarchal, and Louis would have taken him for the young woman's grandfather. Ahead of the sponge, the flesh rippled loosely. Louis's arms went under the cover and made a tent as he worked further down the fevered body. The smell of the body and the smell of the whiskey lifted together.

"I never thought of the Gospel as romance," Louis said. "Though it is that, in a way. Perhaps if you could think of it as the *founding* romance—the romance that was there

before the world was created—the romance that is true—
the one which all other romances signify so imperfectly."

"I have lived my life without heaven," Mr. Alberson
said. "I can die without it."

"You are a man of great daring. Would that your
bravery took the other road."

"If I burn in hell, I burn in hell."

"We've all come short of the glory of God," Louis said
with care. "I pray the Holy Spirit will give you faith to
repent and believe that Christ has suffered our hell for us.
Bizarre as the story is, *repulsive* as it is, this is love, this is
our redemption."

"Not my redemption," Mr. Alberson stated firmly.

"Yes, yours, if you will comply."

Louis was astounded that "*repulsive* as it is" had come
from his mouth. How odd, he thought, that after these
years of being drawn to the altar he should intimate that
the Cross was repulsive. And how very odd that he should
while speaking of the Gospel as romance.

"You seem a fine young man," Mr. Alberson said. His
face changed and became so friendly that Louis thought
grace might have shattered the eyes. Then Louis heard,
"But you are wasting your time."

Unbelief was well in control. There was no delirium in
this sufferer's chamber, of one kind or another.

Louis continued to minister with his hands. "I am here
in the name of Christ. That is all I know. Christ said, 'Go
ye into all the world, and preach the Gospel to every
creature.' For me, at this moment, this room is all the
world." He happened to look out the window. The rain

poured. The house was a solid house, an aristocratic fortress against nature. There was almost no sound of the rain.

Mr. Alberson said, "If you came here to baptize me, dismiss the thought."

The daughter was waiting in the hall.

"I did what I could," Louis told her.

He started back to the Cathedral. A sense of failure hounded him as he walked. The bell began to toll and he gave himself immediately to another sadness, one which was kinder by far. There was no question in his mind, Sister Constance was with her Bridegroom. Mud squashed between the boards in the street. On and on the death rang out through the watery morning.

Sister Clare let him in the sister-house. She looked like a slapped little girl yet to deliver tears, and she was silent to everything he found himself saying. They stood at the foot of the stairs. She held to the newel. She directed toward him the sort of blankness she might have bestowed upon a forward stranger who had wandered in. The last peal faded, seemed to travel off above the trees, and Louis realized that he should lower his voice, maybe even forsake for the moment this business of trying to speak comfort. He wondered if he would ever feel expert at any of the duties to which God had put him.

Down the stairs came Dr. Dalzell.

"You were here with her?" Louis asked him.

"God brought me here in time."

"I'm thankful of that."

Sister Clare got her voice to work. "Yes, the doctor read the commendatory prayer."

Louis said, "I feel I should explain, Father, I was called to a bed in the neighborhood."

Dr. Dalzell looked at him. "Then that is where you should have been. You can't be everywhere at once, Mr. Schuyler."

Now Sister Ruth was descending. "My Sister, I'm useless," she said, "and so ashamed. Mrs. Bullock is robing Sister in her habit and needs help. I'm sorry, it's a grace I don't have."

Sister Clare gathered herself and started up. At one point she turned to them and said, as though a tonic were taking effect, "'Hosanna,' that was her last word, clear as could be."

Louis fed on the thought.

"I'm going out to arrange for a coffin," Dr. Dalzell said. "Pray God it will *be* that, and not a box like many are having to use. I hate to think of that fair person in one of those rough, nailed affairs." He suggested to Sister Ruth that perhaps she would want to write a telegram to Mother Harriet and then prepare the chapel. To Louis he assigned the reading of the service, and suggested that he visit with Dean Harris in the meantime. "I know he is feeling all of this very deeply."

Dr. Dalzell's suggestions came forth with a peaceful authority. It was not simply that here was somebody versed in settling things, but Louis saw a man whose foundation was undisturbed, a man being himself, and heard him establish with a few utterances a firm ground upon which to move and act. Louis prayed that someday he too would possess this quality, and that for now he might learn to like the physician-priest from Louisiana as much as he admired him.

Dean Harris had dressed himself and was almost out of the room when Louis got there. One end of his collar was wild, erect at an angle in the back, and his coat hung loosely, making steep slopes of his shoulders.

Louis stood in the doorway.

"Not Constance," the Dean said.

"The Lord has taken her," Louis said.

"I saw her face at the first sound."

"It was only a matter of time."

"I must go to the others." With obvious determination, the Dean took a step.

"Back to bed for you, Father," Louis said, trying a new voice. "You are not fit. I am certain that Dr. Dalzell would have you remain here and build your strength."

Dean Harris raised his arms in a fashion that might have looked benedictory if his hands had not been fisted. Suddenly Louis expected boxed ears, but then he saw that the fury was trained higher, toward a presence towering them both, toward a personality not so readily visible. The gesture came to nothing. When it wilted, the Dean allowed Louis to turn him around. He went back to bed, clearly spent, shedding only his coat, which he let fall where it would.

Louis picked up the coat and hooded the bedpost. Instead of sitting in the chair beside the bed, he took to the farther one.

Minutes went by with Louis unsure of what to say, and then he found that all he had to do was listen, for the Dean began to recount the worth of the woman who had died—what she had done with the school, how it had grown because of her. The Dean spoke hoarsely now, his debility seeming to intensify the emotion in his words. Everybody, according to him, had been touched by her radiance. She had led the girls in laughter with the same heart that she had led them in prayers. But that was not to suggest slackness, and he indicated how stern she was on occasion. Louis almost got a whiff of chalk and slate. The students having vanished before his arrival, this was the first time he had received a sense of the school as something that had a real life. For that matter, even though he had met her in New York when she was well, this perhaps was the first time he had glimpsed through to more than the *idea* of Sister Constance, to the material of the actual person.

"If I ever saw a woman," the Dean was saying, "whose will it was to do the will of God—"

In the next moments the nun receded, and died again, and became like a seriously-turned-out doll in somebody's attic. It disturbed Louis to realize that he seldom created in his mind a practical flesh with which to mantle the soul of any woman he greatly admired. This was truly a shortcoming for one who claimed to hold a sacramental view. Were all women somehow as incorporeal to him as his mother, whom he had known only as a handed-down memory?

"We go back to Job," he was saying to the Dean. "The Lord gave, and the Lord hath taken away—"

It was not his intention that the verse hang there

unfinished. It occurred to him that Dean Harris might supply the rest of it if he waited and gave him the chance, might let it out as dutifully as one would a response appointed by rubric. But the Dean did not, and Louis had to say it himself. "Blessed be the name of the Lord."

"Why her?" the Dean asked.

"But whom would you have chosen?"

"This is not like me."

"I know, Father."

"Why must the Lord be so hard?"

"It is His way at times," Louis said. He was uncomfortable with the statement, but it seemed the manliest thought he could have expressed. He was feeling older by the minute.

"Pay me no mind," the Dean said. "I'm not as dangerous as I sound."

"I believe that, Father."

"You do?"

"The faith of a child is spoken of, and indeed is required, but I doubt that God despises questions." Louis was beginning to see that faith could balk and argue without loosening its hold. Perhaps, he thought, mature worship commences at a wall of unanswered questions. He would have been willing, almost, to maintain that Christian faith could be as unsentimental as skepticism.

"Who has the funeral?"

"Dr. Dalzell has done me the honor."

Dean Harris gave him a look that for some reason reminded him of blunders in the past, incidents of which the Dean could have no knowledge. The most personal—and the loudest, even now—was the time he had dropped the lavabo bowl, when he was freshly ordained and assisting with the Holy Communion. He wished the Lord would let him forget it forever.

The Dean said, "I suppose you can handle it as well as anybody."

Louis, trying not to note that he had received in the remark less than a thorough investiture, sought a change of subject. He considered telling the Dean about the conversation with Mr. Alberson. He wanted to ask prayers for the man, but he was not in a mood to speak of that unprosperous call. "Shall I read a Psalm before I go?" he asked.

Downstairs, he stole into the Dean's office for paper. He sat at the desk and wrote in a careful hand to his father in St. Louis: *I am so very glad that I came, for I can be of good assistance. Do not worry about me, for I am in God's care. He will allow only what is best for me.*

·11·

THE COFFIN was a piece of work far from shoddy or vulgar. It lay without cloth. The pall had not been found, and there was a little distress about that.

The deep, rubbed black called to the imagination centuries of black. In the geometry itself—in this known thing, in this loaf so explicitly shaped—was a timeless calm which contradicted the haste that had attended procurement. An air trifled with the candles, as though a door to the rain stood open somewhere in the Cathedral. The flames whipped slightly upon their columns. The lid of the coffin reflected the unrest dimly, and seemed, by some innate authority in its blackness, to still the air and bring the flames back to posture.

Louis thanked God that words were given him now. He didn't have to pull them out of himself. He didn't have to pick through scripture and strain for the guidance of the Spirit, didn't have to thumb here and there and fan pages at the bereaved company, didn't have to depend on prayers from the top of his head. Open in his hand was a

93

solid gift of the Church—or, as he thought of it at this moment, a gift from God *to* the Church, for a distilled grammar of faith and practice. The Book of Common Prayer might not include all of the offices he thought important, but its treasure was great and always ready. Who could improve The Order for the Burial of the Dead? He was sure that, left to his own formulations, he would reduce the service to confusion. He had witnessed an undisciplined funeral once, long ago, that of a boy he had liked very much, and he had grieved for more than the loss of a friend.

> *I am the resurrection and the life, saith the Lord: he that believeth in me, though he were dead, yet shall he live: and whosoever liveth and believeth in me shall never die.*

His gaze went out to the faces there, and again to the coffin. Then, for security, he brought his eyes back to the print. What he knew by heart would not be insulted or depreciated by his using that which was visible. Why should he try to impress anybody?

> *I know that my Redeemer liveth, and that he shall stand at the latter day upon the earth. And though after my skin worms destroy this body, yet in my flesh shall I see God: whom I shall see for myself, and mine eyes shall behold, and not another.*

> *We brought nothing into this world, and it is certain we can carry nothing out. The Lord gave—*

He realized he was not reading for the death of Sister Constance alone. Death could never be narrowed to a singularity. He was taking Father Parsons into account, and strangers dying even now, and the woman he would have called Mother if she had lived, and the boy he had liked long ago. And he was reading for deaths yet to come, for deaths waiting to be born. These words embraced the whole ancestral cup passed down from the days in the garden. Sister Constance was but a case in point.

Exercising one choice that was his, Louis settled for Psalm 90.

Lord, thou hast been our refuge—

He always felt the power of this Psalm. He loved the taste of the phrases in his mouth. Each thought deserved its proper music, each punctuation mark its proper silence. But he found, on towards the end, that he was rushing along in anticipation of the Lesson.

Ah, the Lesson. Here was the *other* cup, for all who would drink of it.

Now is Christ risen from the dead, and become the first-fruits of them that slept. For since by man came death, by man came also the resurrection of the dead. For as in Adam all die, even so in Christ shall all be made alive. But every man in his own order—

Besides Louis and Dr. Dalzell, only two men were present. They sat on the opposite side from the Sisters and

Mrs. Bullock, a row back. Louis had never seen them before. He took it simply that they were strangers sent from God to help with the load. He had wondered if he and Dr. Dalzell could manage the coffin decently to the wagon, and the idea of a hunt for men up and down the streets was abhorrent to him. The streets were mostly deserted anyway. But there was no predicament. The two, without waiting for signal or plea, stepped forward when Dr. Dalzell did, and the four of them found holds and lifted, and carried their communal burden slowly out and into the rain.

It was the first time Louis had ever participated in the physical chore necessary at every funeral. The weight pulled at his shoulder, suggested to his back the ache that the floor had worked into him during the night. The discomfort now was almost a satisfying thing. It had to do with being a man. It was sensual. It brought his perception sharply to the reality of what he and the other bearers were about. And it did make a difference. Having performed the spiritual service, and having taken care of that aspect a number of times before, Louis thought it meet that for once he come to terms with the hard-surfaced business of the matter.

The rain bounced on the wood, the drops tapping a hollow rhythm. The mud underfoot could not be avoided. Louis placed his feet where they had to go. When the coffin was in the wagon, the two strangers climbed to the seat. Then the rest of the party got to the buggies, Dr. Dalzell helping Sister Ruth and Sister Frances into his, Louis helping Sister Clare and Mrs. Bullock into the other one, the second and last in line. Louis stepped up and, claiming the reins, sat tightly to his side, trying not to mash Sister Clare, who sat in the middle. Mrs. Bullock sat forward, practically off the seat, doing her part to ease the crowded situation.

The wagon started. The first buggy followed in the ruts. Louis hoped the coffin wouldn't wobble and lurch about. After he had set his horse to motion, he happened to look to the window of Sister Hughetta's room. There she was, her face at the sill, with another Sister leaning near. It seemed that the patient had been allowed without wrangle to watch the procession off, for the mood between her and the nurse appeared peaceful enough and one of mutual support. The picture was that of children kept from a grown-up affair. The glimpse of them, removed as they were, caught his thoughts to others who if possible would have joined the train. He gave mind to Sister Thecla and the Sister who attended her—the window there was vacant, and that no doubt was best—and to Dean Harris over in his residence, grudgingly obedient, whose window could not be seen from the street. He then contemplated the Sisters of St. Mary far away in Peekskill, and especially Mother Harriet. In the same way that Mr. Parsons' death had come to him most vividly in the remembered face of Mrs. Moffat, this death increased in power when he saw the Superior looming before him. So few days had gone by since their morning walk together. She had received a telegram that day, she had received a telegram this day. Now she was like a grand and imposing statue, but with eyes welling, eyes as human as sorrow. Her countenance came to him wetly, as though the rain were its agent.

Soon the procession was passing the Alberson house.

He told his passengers of his visit with Mr. Alberson. They perked with interest, setting their mourning aside for the time. They knew of the man, had long been concerned about him—knew of him mostly through his daughter, of course, but they said it was common knowledge that, although he gave generously to the school, he exulted in his skepticism. Such a pity, they said.

As the buggy was crawling on toward the end of the block, Louis heard a voice calling him. He looked over his shoulder and saw Mr. Alberson's daughter. She had come out and was whisking along, trailing the buggy down the middle of the street, skirts hoisted wisely but not entirely escaping the mud.

He stopped the horse and walked back to talk with her.

"Who is gone?" she asked.

He said the name.

She covered her face and gave the death a moment of silence. She asked him to convey her sympathy to the Sisters. Then she apologized for delaying him, and mentioned, hardly as an afterthought, that her father was growing worse. She said something about black vomit. "I would be so pleased if you could visit with him again when you return from the cemetery. He's *asking* for a clergyman now. I don't think he even remembers that you were there this morning."

"This burying can be done without me," Louis said. "Wait. I'll run ahead and speak with Dr. Dalzell. Mrs. Bullock will be happy to drive." He felt absolutely no guilt in his decision to excuse himself from the trek to the cemetery. He was needed by one yet living, one much needier than Sister Constance. He did feel it was an undeserved blessing, though, that he would be permitted to evade the dolor and inconvenience of rites at a muddy grave-mouth.

"Bring me a man of God," Mr. Alberson said.

"I am here," Louis assured him.

"You sound like a Yankee. You're no man of God. First you come to kill us, then you come to save us."

"Sir, I believe the fever is confusing you. I am from the Cathedral. I was here this morning. Don't you remember?"

"I am not confused." The man's head hung from the side of the bed, toward a chamber pot that reeked. "*He* was here, not you."

He?

It was not a time to contend a point. Louis said, "I am here now and I would like to help you if I can."

"You say you're a preacher?"

"Yes, a priest."

There came a violent spew. Louis had to close his eyes until the sounds of it were over.

Mr. Alberson, when he could speak again, said, "Something has happened—this *Christ*—I think you will be interested." Every breath he took came back as a moan. "All my life I've been fighting Him off, giving Him hell— and then He comes to me, forces Himself into my room when I'm helpless, touches me, bathes me with cool whiskey—I don't have an out anymore—"

Louis was filling with a kind of terror, as dizzying as the fumes from the chamber pot. He wanted, for the sake of fact, to tell him that it wasn't exactly Christ who had visited him earlier. But was the truth in the man's confusion larger and more important than a restricting accuracy? He sat down on the edge of the bed. His instruction in the mystery of the Incarnation had not prepared him for this jolt. Although he was afraid he would honor himself too highly if he didn't clarify things, he certainly didn't want to belittle the Presence by disclaiming it in any way.

"Thanks be to God," he said, for something to express.

"I didn't recognize Him until He was gone—but then I knew—"

"I hope your confession doesn't rest solely on what might have seemed a miraculous appearance."

"Don't try to talk me out of it!"

"You misunderstand me. I would only explain that believing matters more than seeing."

"I have swallowed the Cross—what else can I tell you?—the damned wood is in my throat right now."

The language was not orthodox and the conversation itself was somewhat irregular, but Louis thought that enough had been professed to more than compensate for Mr. Alberson's lack of instruction in repentance and faith. He recalled that many of the stories of Christ were completely void of gentility.

"Do you desire to be baptized?"

"Why the devil do you wait?" Mr. Alberson said.

Louis went to the daughter and requested a bowl of fresh water.

She reached out to fend off the wall when it got in her way. Then she was going down the stairs, her skirts chanting to the still house. Louis followed her. He wanted a while to breathe. Compared to the room, the hall was like an airy pavilion.

·12·

IT RAINED all day. It rained all day the next day, and on and on. It would let up to a drizzle and then a new wave would come flailing. The drench got so tiresome that Louis stopped trying to connect it with a pouring of grace. The rain was nothing but unholy, miserable rain.

He refused, though, to let the dreary weather discourage him in his course of mission. Holding fast to the idea that Heaven had blessed his efforts with Mr. Alberson, he answered call after call. He felt like a dripping spaniel everywhere he went. Sometimes he would not get back to the Cathedral before he was beckoned in another direction. Dr. Dalzell warned him not to go into the deeper parts of the town, the neighborhoods where the pestilence was the thickest, but how was one to know where "the deeper parts" began? It was impossible to draw a line when streets were unfamiliar and somebody came for help and led the way.

Each house was a test. He never knew quite what to do. In houses of parishioners he could resort with good conscience to The Order for the Visitation of the Sick, even when the office seemed an unhelpful interference in a death vigil. But he found himself in alien situations where God apparently was not of the essence at all, where to speak of Christ or merely read a Psalm was to fight in vain. He had to remind himself that if he could not minister Christ to these people, his duty was to minister *to Christ*, whether he could detect Him or not. "Inasmuch as ye have done it unto the least of these my brethren," He had said, "ye have done it unto me."

One day he encountered the red-haired nurse he had seen on the train. His recognition of her turned his thoughts to the younger nurse, the one who had ridden opposite him. If he were to see her again, he would take her aside from her duties for a moment of quiet and courteous introduction. Perhaps he would offer his shoulder for a rest for her head. He was certain that they would draw strength from each other. He inquired about her, and the woman told him she thought the "girl" was nursing at one of the infirmaries downtown.

It was in a fine old house that he talked with the woman. Silver in an open trunk made him suspect that she was up to looting, but there was no way for him to prove it or do anything about it.

In a district of closed businesses, at a corner high on a bluff overlooking the river, he found a warehouse that was serving as an infirmary. Nobody sent for him—he went there by choice, sniffing his way on his own. The doctor in charge, after warning him that there were no empty cots if he happened to fall sick while on the premises, allowed him to wander through. The walls had been tarred and the floors had been swabbed with lime, as disinfectant measures, but not every inch was covered and Louis was struck by the harlequin result in this place where the goings-on were so out of step with buffoonery.

The first ward was for men. He went to each cot, ready with a prayer. Some of the patients welcomed him and some did not. "How many did the sharpshooter get today?" a wizened character wanted to know. It caught Louis off guard, but he understood too well that the man was asking about the latest count. *How many did God kill today? God the sharpshooter!* The unguessable arithmetic was not the actual point of the question, and Louis knew it. He said, "Those of us who trust Him call Him by a different name." For that man, he composed a special prayer and offered it silently.

Separating the men's ward from the women's ward was a clothesline draped with quilts and a long swag of bunting that had been used in some political festivity of the past. Louis stuck his head through the opening. A nurse—he noticed immediately that she was not the one he sought—came forward and invited him in. After seeing him to the nearest patient, she went on down the row, attempting to make concealments of flesh, and here and there banishing receptacles, in preparation for his tour of the area. The other nurses busied themselves, and none was the one he sought. He tried to keep his mind on his visits, on his prayers, but he looked for that face every time he looked up.

When he came to the last patient, something drove at his

heart. A closer look told him that he was mistaken. His eyes had sported with him, the face was not the face he had thought. His relief was as great as his disappointment. The emotions could not be extracted one from the other. It turned out that the young woman who lay there was of the communion, had been raised in the Church, *wanted* him to open his Prayer Book. So it was a pleasant visit anyhow, as pleasant as possible under the circumstances.

The doctor in charge followed him outside. Had Louis been to Annie Cook's Mansion House? It was a demimonde establishment down on Gayoso Street, the doctor explained, and although it was a place a man of the cloth would not ordinarily go, he might very well want to pay a call there at this time because it was known that Annie had turned her place into a hospital, had released her girls, some of whom had stayed on to nurse.

If a man of the cloth could find it in his heart to go—the doctor was pointing in the direction, a route parallel to the river landing—would he please talk sense into the girl named Fern? "She must get out of town while there's time. Tell her that Dr. Bob doesn't want her to die. She can go out in the country to my family's plantation, away from this poison. She can tell them she's a schoolteacher, she can tell them anything, it will be all right. I'm sending my nigger to pick her up at six this evening. He'll be waiting at the door."

Louis was without a buggy that day. He was tired. He had thought he would go back to the Cathedral, but he changed his mind and walked in the direction the doctor had indicated. The street kept to the lofted shoulder of the river. Except for an old packet rotting down there at the water's edge, the landing was entirely forsaken. Buggies and wagons, the few that were on the street, moved along in as brisk a fashion as the mud would permit. Now and then a pedestrian appeared at a distance, and disappeared. Louis was becoming so used to the seeming unreality of everything that he was hardly shocked by the thought of where he was heading. The world had tilted and all the fixtures had slipped from their assigned moorings. Louis Schuyler was on his way to a bagnio. So? Who was Louis Schuyler to set bounds on the Lord's interest? But he wondered about delivering the personal message to the girl named Fern. What was of Christ and what wasn't? Would an act of kindness ever be *not* of Christ? A favor to a sinner and a favor to sin were two different things, surely. The real problem was whether or not he should encourage a person to think of self when others were in need.

He found the place easily, in spite of the fact that the doctor had not given him the street number. There was an aura about the front. Something in the comradely file of hitching posts defied the staidness of the entrance. It might be true that the character of the house had altered because of the epidemic, but Louis thought he would have suspected, even in normal times, that here, behind the facade, behind this curtain of respectable white paint, were rooms set apart for commerce in the most fleshly of mysteries. The woman who answered his knock was around the age of Mother Harriet, and in her own way she was every bit as official-looking. Her gaze fell immediately to his cross.

"This is—unexpected," she said, stepping outside to

talk with him. "You must be a stranger to Memphis. You wouldn't have come here."

"I try to follow the Lord wherever He leads," Louis said. "I understand that you have patients at this address."

"My name is Annie Cook. I should tell you that my house—has a reputation. A plague doesn't do much to change the color of that."

"I have come with prayers, not stones."

Annie Cook was looking into his eyes now. "Your prayers are welcome and so very needed, but you would be criticized by many people if it ever got about that you set foot in this house."

Louis opened the door and waited for Annie Cook to precede him.

The sitting-room into which she conducted him was empty of other people. Central and suspended like doom was an unlighted chandelier that impressed Louis as too large for its domain. The prisms hung like a crown of stilled rain, dusty, refracting but scraggly cheer in the afternoon darkness. The chairs and sofas were backed against the walls, as though to avoid a splash. If he would have a seat, she said, she would inquire in the rooms to see if anyone desired a call. It was clear that privacy was always to be respected in her business. He sat near the archway where she disappeared. When he thought he heard her returning, the footsteps stopped short. He looked up and found that a young woman was peeping from behind the arch.

"Are you Fern?" he asked the eye.

The other eye appeared and a wisp of ivory hair dipped farther into the room. "I'm Cora. Do you know Fern?"

"No, but I bring a message to her. Perhaps when she has a moment."

The eyes registered a profound curiosity and then took leave. Louis heard Annie Cook tell somebody, maybe Cora in passing, to make a pot of tea. He was still looking toward the archway when the madam entered. She motioned for him not to rise.

She had been unsuccessful in preparing a way for him, and was apologetic, saying that nobody was inclined, that all of them were very shy. She gave a gesture which seemed to confide that she had been dealing with obstinate children. Would he stay for a cup of tea? She sat down, two chairs from his. She herself was feeling poorly, she told him, and she thought she would drink a cup of tea and give up and go to bed. He was not to look so concerned, *please.* God owed her no favors.

He asked, "May I take this opportunity—?"

Annie Cook did nothing to forestall him. She simply touched her forehead. She might have been singling out a pain.

"God owes favors to none of us," Louis said. "Only by His mercy do we become recipients, whatever our deeds. You are caught up in a motion of grace already. This is evident in the charity you are performing. I would entreat you to change this house *further*—to *hallow* it—by casting yourself at the feet of the Savior, the One who has chosen you."

"What kind of sermon is this?" Annie Cook said. "I believe you *are* naive. I grew up on fire and brimstone."

"Would you prefer? The other side is there."

"I could resist you better."

It was almost as if they were courting, but Annie Cook kept a somber face. White finger marks lingered on her forehead when her hand moved from there to the tray Cora brought.

She poured for Louis.

When she was settling down with her own cup, she seemed not to arrive at a solid cushion, but swayed unanchored for a moment, her tea spilling, and suddenly it appeared that the cup was too heavy and was pulling her forward and down to the floor. Louis was not quick enough to receive her. Before he could put his tea aside, some of it sloshed to her hair. The stains on the floor widened hurriedly and came together beyond her head.

Cora was out of the room. The sounds of upset, some of which Louis had contributed vocally, brought her back. She spoke to Annie. She crawled around her, accomplishing nothing. Annie was still in a faint. Louis gathered her up, and, with Cora leading, carried her through the archway. Louis remembered the pictures of the Shepherd carrying the sheep. The madam, in the arms of Louis Schuyler, was not so containable a charge.

Rooms went by him like dusky cells passing an absorbed abbot. From one of them came another young woman, a Negress, open-mouthed but silent as a fish, who joined the mortal procession. When a bed was before him, and even as the counterpane peeled back windily, he let the weight down.

Annie began to moan. She opened her eyes. "What happened?" she said.

Cora leaned over one side of the bed, the Negress over the other side. They were telling her what good nursing she was going to get, and that she was going to be all right. A girl Louis had not seen before, a girl with freckles, who looked no older than fifteen or sixteen, had come in and was straightening the counterpane at the foot. Louis realized that his time with Annie Cook was gone. Female hands had taken over. His little sermon was unfinished, but ended. He would have to leave her to those hands, and to God.

He took a direct path down the corridor, reminding himself of the choice that Annie had given her patients. If a voice from a room called out to him, he would enter, but not a voice came, except that of a man bawling for Cora to come and fan him. When he found the room with the chandelier, he stooped and retrieved the cup from the floor. The cup surprised him, was still of one piece, could be used for years if handled with caution. Whimsically, he wondered if it might preserve in its bell shape an echo of this day.

"I'm Fern." The girl with the freckles had followed him. Her hands were offering to take the cup. "Cora said that you have a message for me."

"Fern, my child," Louis said, and heard an old man talking, "do you know a Dr. Bob?"

"He's dead?" she asked.

"He wasn't when I saw him a short while ago." Louis told her the doctor's wishes. He told her without adding any persuasion of his own.

She was looking into the cup, as though her decision might be forming there.

Louis took out his watch. It was five minutes past six. He and the girl went to the window, and the secretive blinds revealed stripes of the scene on Gayoso Street. Instead of rain, sunlight poured, and the mud was bright. A wagon was waiting. The driver looked straight ahead, the set of his shoulders expressing a lifetime of long waits.

"I'm not going anywhere," Fern said. "It doesn't do any good to run from God. He catches up with you sooner or later, wherever you go. That was the first thing I thought about when Cora said a man wearing a cross was here."

"There is truth in what you say. But God is our life. It is life that He brings us, even in death, if we will forsake the devil and receive the gift of faith."

"The gift? You make it sound like a trinket, a pretty."

"God help me, I don't mean to," Louis said. "It is anything but that. The gift is Christ Himself. He is love and He is the lover."

"You're not talking to an innocent little girl. I can tell you things that would turn you red as an apple. Christ would have nothing to do with me."

Louis thought of a language that might reach her. He lifted his cross. With it, he divided her face into four sections. He said, "Christ has *bought* you. Think on that."

Fern ducked. Then she went all the way down on her knees. Before Louis could stop her, she began to brush cakes of drying earth from his trouser-bottoms. Her hair, thrown forward, billowed beneath his hands. He was embarrassed by the servile attention, almost frightened by it. His hands were perspiring.

He said, "I would say to you what Christ said to someone a long time ago, 'Go and sin no more.'"

"Go to the country?"

"Not unless you want to, no."

"I think I'd rather God catch me holding heads and emptying slop jars," she said, "than out in the country telling lies to Dr. Bob's family."

"You have my admiration," Louis said, retreating toward the entrance. "I shall tell the driver not to wait."

When the driver learned that Fern was not coming, and that Louis was on foot and bound for the Cathedral, he offered him a ride. He was toothless and his words required a certain fancy on the part of the hearer. Louis stepped up and sat on the board beside him. Turning for a last look at Annie Cook's Mansion House, he saw a pigeon with a healthy coat strutting on the roof. He wondered if it might be a sign. Was the Spirit of God wearing nature once again? It was heartening to remember that God was the God of Rahab and the God of the Magdalene. Louis would have taken nothing in exchange for his belief in miracles.

But after a while the wagon began to pound rationality up his spine and into his head, dulling the edge of faith. He had doubts about his ministry to Annie and the girl. He should have said more, he should have said less, he should have stayed longer, he never should have gone to that place at all. The only thing he could tell himself for sure was that Louis Schuyler had visited a bagnio, a *whorehouse,* in the name of Christ. He hated his doubts and tried to fight them off. He didn't want the Redemption to shrink to the measly proportions of *his* ability, or miracles to evaporate into tired old dreams. He thought about Mr. Alberson's madness. It was unlikely that anybody else would be dealt such a vision. But the truth was—and God knew it—he had liked the harlots, even those with whom he hadn't had a chance, better than he had liked Mr. Alberson. Now that he thought about it, he knew that he had recognized in them at least remnants of the young nurse he remembered from the train.

The western sun bounced off the river and steamed on his back. Summer had not been washed away. Until frost there was no hope of the fever leaving town. The driver was a born conversationalist, but now and then he lapsed into an unknown tongue and it was impossible to tell whether he was relating death beyond description or making a fervent noise unto the Lord.

Sister Ruth called Louis out to see the sunset. He had finished the egg that was supper. They went out to the street for the view, where the trees were not a hindrance, where the way was straight to the fire.

"The glory of the Lord shall be revealed," Sister Ruth said, in awe.

"And to think we see darkly here," Louis said.

"It's only a matter of time for Sister Thecla."

Louis knew that Sister Ruth was not changing the subject. "It's only a matter of time for each of us," he said.

Upon his return that afternoon, he had learned that Sister Clare and Mrs. Bullock were down with the fever. They had fallen ill within an hour of each other. It was as if an archer were closing in on the camp.

"We must not grow despondent, Father. Dean Harris is improving daily, and Sister Hughetta's case doesn't seem as bad as some. Sister Frances is looking unwell, I know, but she assures me nothing is wrong."

"I am not despondent. But still, someday, for each of us, the hour will come."

Although the river could not be seen from where they stood, the sky seemed to carry the flow above the horizon, and one might have imagined that the body of water was the furnace in which the clouds were being consumed.

It was good to lie down. He hoped that sleep would rush over him. He lay with his arms stretched flat and straight out. There was no rug in that corner of the parlor, only the blankets on which he lay, and his hands were against wood. Soon he realized that his position was like that of the eleventh Station of the Cross—not the prone genuflection of the devotional step but the authentic and literal attitude, facing heaven for the nailing. He raised a knee, but he still felt the similarity—*saw* it, as though from a point outside himself. Repelled, he let his knee fall to the side. The abandon was delicious. It was good to be alive, to be of flesh, to have a body capable of appreciating the smallest tactile pleasure. Even a cotton sheet carelessly brushing a leg could make a man want to taste every mystery but death. His thoughts were not free of the afflictions about, but it seemed that his tissue was defying all of that. He supposed the spectacle of Memphis had brought him down to the simple, primitive luxury of existence itself. He raised the knee again, and let it fall again. But then, as though from that point outside himself, he saw the movement as a mockery of writhing, so he stopped it.

·13·

ON SCRAPS of paper stuffed in his pockets were names and street numbers given him by individuals who had mentioned concern for this or that friend or relative. Often as not he found himself at a door where his knocking went unanswered. He would assume that the inhabitants had locked up and left town, but there nagged at him each time the possibility that inside was somebody too weak to appear. And then, on the other hand, he was aware that a clerical collar and intentions of mercy did not guarantee entrance even where trouble was. Some families had sealed themselves off, and, for fear of infection, would open to no one. Once—was it yesterday or the day before?—a man's voice had threatened from an upstairs window and Louis had seen a gun parting the curtains.

Now he came to a house on Vance Avenue, to call on a Miss Randolph. The door stood open, thrown wide in the warm-weather custom of genial neighborhoods, and this surprised Louis despite the summer that was holding on.

He peered into the hallway as he knocked. Memories of a sane world swam around, floated up and down the stairs. Louis was thirsty. He decided he would ask his hostess for a drink of water. If she lay ill, he would take the liberty of serving himself. He knocked again. Amber from the fanlight polished the hat-rack's wood antlers and shone in its mirror. Louis felt curiously invited, although his welcome remained spectral and voiceless.

He went in and waited at the foot of the stairs.

"Miss Randolph?" he called.

He was not an intruder, he told himself.

To the right was the parlor. A piano was partly visible, and when Louis saw it he could see little else. It did to the space and the objects of the room what a waiting ship might do to a port when a sailor has been ashore too long. He was tempted to go into the room, to the yellowed ivory, to the soft black, and let his fingers quietly pay respects. But his purpose in trespassing kept him balanced, and he went on to the doors down the passage.

"Miss Randolph?"

The house was not in perfect order, and who would have expected it to be? The rooms reflected a gracious life nonetheless, even if a breathing presence of it was not to be found.

He gave himself a moment in the kitchen. The water was shallow and tasted of the bucket, but his throat demanded more than one swallow. The walls exuded a bouquet of cooking from the past, with the flavors fused into one indefinite smell, a richness now dried. His stomach rebelled against the thought of food. His thirst had nothing to do with hunger. He wondered if he would ever be hungry again.

He walked to the front and started up the stairs. It was unbelievable that the place had been abandoned in this vulnerable condition. And yet it made no difference, he didn't like the idea of what he was doing. By what authority was he violating the privacy of these quarters?

Climbing toward that other silence, his mind went back to Peekskill, back where faith had seemed harmless and the will of God as irre. .ible as a waltz. He was not so simple-minded now—or perhaps he was, for here he trod. The board in a step near the top sighed and then sang out, and sighed again as he lifted his weight. A heart set on melody was not to be outdone, he supposed. He had always responded to the violins in old houses, and only a boor would have called the sound a squeak.

But now was no time for music.

"Miss Randolph?"

He practically tiptoed on his search of the second level, inhaling and exhaling as if he had taken the stairs at a run. His head was beginning to throb. He discovered not a soul—only a bed, the covers tossed down, the pillow dimpled.

That the bed was unoccupied neither relieved nor disturbed him. He stood and looked at it, his emotions numb. He tried to care as he had cared up to now. He studied the woman who was absent, whom he didn't know, whose contours the linen remembered. He was tired and he wanted to escape his head. He reached out and touched where the softness was rampant. His knees followed. Shocked at the outrage he was committing, he buried his cheek. The feathery arms of the mattress came about him deeply.

He slept.

When he pulled himself up, he had to deal with his head again. The commotion in the flowered wall fairly drove him from the room. The house and its riddle came back to him as he descended the stairs. Then everything faded once more, everything but the piano.

He sat down and washed his hands together in the air above the keyboard. The Lord wouldn't have the world all clouds and despair, so why not some sprightly Chopin? There was the troublesome matter of the headache, and his fingers felt thick and slow, but the Lord could lift him above petty hindrances. And besides, when a gentleman was prevailed upon to play, did a gentleman cower and hide and make excuses? Why was he stalling? Fumbles would be forgivable. It seemed ages since he had had a chance to practice.

With a sudden fall, he went into the mazurka that his father loved. Louis had never set out to memorize the piece, but it was requested so often at home, and at parties too, that one day he had realized it was a part of him. He could almost believe his father was listening now, nodding a smile to a book. Any house with music, in whatever town, was somehow in the country of home, Louis thought. He had decided, as a boy, that music came down from heaven and went back there when the sound died. He had never really tried to put the fancy away. He saw no theological conflict in it. Wasn't heaven the storehouse of every delight that wasn't a lie? Honor to the composer—to the poet, to the artist—was not lessened. Chopin, unless he was a terribly arrogant fellow, would not have minded being called a vessel of God.

The mazurka was not going well today, though. It became like a thing whipping in a gale. It tugged Louis over rough places, one stone after another, yet it was hardly the dance which God and Chopin had ordained. He finally chose to let it go.

He was embarrassed when he looked up and saw Winifred Pell sitting there by the window. He had forgotten that he had an audience. He had even forgotten that he was in New York.

Winifred Pell was waiting patiently for Handel's *Largo*. And she would have it, he resolved.

"For you," he said, and his caution in planting the first chord was similar to that of a man at chess.

A broad column of sound rose from the landscape within him. The sedate mood of this piece would calm him and soothe his head, he hoped. He closed his eyes, trusting his fingers to lead him correctly from one chord to the next. It was interesting that Winifred Pell's taste would run to something so contemplative and bare of frills. He had thought of her, though a widow and older than he, mainly as a girl. He had thought of her as a very pretty girl, more bubble than substance. But there was no telling what profound reservoirs lay hushed beneath the shimmer of that charm. Were he to explore the mysterious region where her inner life took its course, would he ever return?

Most of the chords were acceptable. He got to the last one. The silence came and he opened his eyes. Mrs. Pell sat in absolute repose, with her hair crushed against the chair-back. It appeared that she had been lulled to sleep.

Louis was not offended in the least. It was a compliment—like an intimate gift, he thought—that she had yielded so thoroughly to his playing.

Although he felt it was time to depart, he hated to slip away without a word. He had a notion to wake her with a kiss. For an instant he was aware of no restrictions at all, but then his inexperience became a burden to him, and he had to drop the idea as he approached her chair. His head weighed enough as it was. He reached out to touch her hand, and hesitated. He saw for the first time that she was wearing a gown for bed. The silken folds melted thinly and nothing fettered her breasts. How had he stumbled over this border? In what ancient meadow, or in what Cathedral was he worshipping now? Was he looking upon beauty or upon something even more consuming? Here was Eve, here was Bathsheba, here was the Shulamite, here was the young nurse he had admired on the train. The memory of the train jarred him. He was in Memphis, not in New York. This was the town of Annie Cook and her girls. These breasts couldn't belong to Winifred Pell. He pulled almost up and discovered the saffron face of a stranger. He caught at her shoulder for poise, and she tipped to the side and tottered there, chilling the parlor, a corpse with the springiness of a live carrot.

·14·

"ARE YOU NOT feeling well?" Dean Harris asked.

"It's nothing," Louis said. He was in the Dean's room, but he couldn't remember why. "I believe I'm having one of my spells, that's all. I hope that you will not think less of me."

"Spells? Everyone is entitled to a spell now and then, especially under present conditions. Tell me no more of the town. Go ahead and weep. I shall weep with you."

"I would appreciate your not mentioning to Dr. Dalzell the tenuous hold I have on my emotions."

"He is with us now," the Dean said softly. He looked beyond Louis, toward the door. "Doctor," he said, "you must see that our brother gets some rest. He has been working too hard."

The hand that touched Louis's forehead might have come from snow. The cold of the fingers caused him to draw back. The hand followed and pressed for a moment longer. The doctor was frowning.

"Open up," the doctor said.

Louis opened his mouth to remonstrate. A thumb and a finger took his chin and forced a wider gap. His tongue felt very naked as the doctor's eyes came close for an investigation.

"I am so sorry, Mr. Schuyler," Louis heard, and he knew that those words implied a diagnosis.

"But it's only a spell," he said. "It will pass. I shall be all right."

"Call it what you wish," the doctor said, "you have the yellow fever."

Every article in the room whirled in confusion around the statement, and only the statement was absolutely quiet and solid.

"But my work is not over," Louis said.

"For now it is," the doctor said.

"There's a house I must visit. I went there the day I arrived, but I was afraid to go in. A child is alone there. I must go back and help. I have the heart to do it now."

Dean Harris said, "Do not be ashamed of your tears. You are crying the tears of a man."

The doctor said to the Dean, "Though he cry the tears of Christ, I must get him to a bed."

Louis had a vision then. He saw a family of rats feasting, and the horror of it was so strong that it calmed him, as a blow to his head would have calmed him. There was no need to go back for the boy. It was too late to help. Time had performed its service. The thought of this—the thought of his complicity in it—delivered Louis to a place of mind darker than he had ever imagined, where it seemed to him that the Redemption should have no hold. He had a strange sense of homecoming, although he had never stood on this land before. Perhaps he had lived without the *pain* of debt as long as he could. His rightful communion was with cowards. And with murderers.

The doctor was trying to steer him out of the room, saying something about an infirmary on Court Street, a facility that had been set up for the care of stricken physicians and nurses. He was saying he thought he could persuade the doctor in charge to take Louis in. "He's a man from Texas, highly qualified, supposed to know what he is doing."

Louis looked at Dean Harris. "Please, I would like to remain near the Cathedral."

"We must do what Dr. Dalzell thinks best," the Dean said.

"There will be no more camping in the parlor," Dr. Dalzell made clear.

"My things," Louis said, turning from the buggy.

"Wait here, I'll get them," the doctor said.

Sister Frances drove up while Louis was standing there by the street. Louis regretted not paying a visit to the orphan asylum, not doing something to lighten her work. As it was, they were scarcely acquainted with each other, most of their time together having been confined to the Eucharist. Now he offered his hand to help her down. More than gallantry prompted him. In that civil gesture, with only fingers embracing, and without a show of the drama inside him, he reached out to her as to a mother, for protection, desperately hoping that she would plead his case and do something to prevent what was happening.

"How are the children?" he asked, and he thought

about the child who wasn't there, who should have been.

"We have escaped so far, thank the Lord," Sister Frances said. "How are my Sisters today?"

Her feet touched the ground and immediately took the walk for the sister-house. Louis was losing his opportunity to tell her of his own plight. Dr. Dalzell, clutching the travelling bag, was coming out of the Dean's residence. Louis noticed that the bag was not shut to. A pair of his underdrawers protruded.

Sister Frances was saying something to the side. "—I have a boy of twelve who needs the hand of a man, should one of you get a chance. He torments the goose every time I turn my back, and this morning he put pepper in the babies' mouths." She was almost in the door and was not waiting for a reply.

"I shall come out to help you," Louis called.

The doctor was kind about it, did not contradict him.

Louis looked at the Cathedral. "Might I be allowed to celebrate the Holy Communion one more time?"

"Into the buggy, Mr. Schuyler."

Louis said, "Lord, I have loved the habitation of thy house, and the place where thine honor dwelleth."

A hand was at his back. "Up—!"

Louis had heard the inflection somewhere before. *A man in the circus was holding a hoop. A dog was about to jump through it.*

When the boost was completed and Louis was sitting with the bag in his lap, the doctor hopped to the driver's seat and took the reins. He promised Louis that he would bring the Sacrament every day.

"If you would," Louis said.

"Yes, of course."

The wooden cathedral had fallen behind.

"I wanted to serve the Lord."

"You *have* served the Lord."

"These spells—this weakness of mine—why am I cursed so? I was rejected from Cowley St. John because of my peculiar problem, and now I am rejected from the Lord's work here, for the same reason."

Louis was surprised at himself. He had always found it extremely difficult to discuss with anybody the matter of his embarrassing attacks. He had discussed the burden with him*self* as little as possible. Now he was speaking of it openly.

"I know nothing of your health at the monastery," the doctor said. "I know nothing of your history, nothing of God's purpose in your life. But I do know the yellow jack when I see it."

"You think I am burning with fever. On the contrary, believe me, I am freezing at this very moment."

"Yes, that is how it is at times."

Louis let the argument pass. It was almost a relief to think that this might not be the old disorder. The "nervous condition" had held off for months, and perhaps he really was over it, perhaps God had answered his prayers. With this hope, he could face the idea of a new and unbelievable enemy.

But why would God remove a thorn and send a spear?

What kind of mercy was that?

Now and then the branches of the trees bordering the way came together above the buggy. How handsome the trees would be when autumn fell. Not a red or a gold had touched yet. Suspended between him and the light, in those moments when the buggy passed through the arches, were myriads of veins, drying, and myriads of leaf-points, waiting. The glory of God was waiting for the glory of God.

Perhaps the mercy of God was waiting for the mercy of God.

The thought consoled Louis, then perplexed him.

God had called him to Memphis and he had obeyed, but what had been accomplished? Was it a sin to wonder? He had known that he was exposing himself to danger, and in one respect he had given his life away before he came, but he had trusted God to shield him and employ him in some useful manner. The act of obedience, which had loosed him from sense and notion, and which for a time had seemed to free him from both the past and the future, could not be reversed. He had given his heart, and it was too late to take it back. Now he was being thrust off, discarded, and he had to believe, if he believed anything at all, that God was behind it, God was *in* it. This was the God who loved him? This was the God he had worshipped? The unchangeable God who never slackened in purpose?

A mattress smouldered in the gutter. The incense was pungent, and Louis held his breath until the cloud had passed. He saw a gate where a body lay wrapped in a cloth as white and unsoiled as altar linen, lay unattended, waiting for the city wagon. On they rode, and Dr. Dalzell was singing the hymn, "Crown Him with Many Crowns." He was singing in a low voice, in a reverent but absent-minded fashion, and the hymn was subject to the rhythm of the buggy. It seemed to Louis that the song of praise was sorely out of appointment with the time and the place. God was in His sanctuary. God was not here.

Why had He deserted Memphis? And why should He wait and return in crystals of frost? Why should He not come back today and work healing with a gentle wind? Had the people committed transgressions so extraordinary that they merited such punishment? Louis doubted it. Yet he remembered the cities of the plain and the other biblical instances in which entire social orders had fallen from grace. He granted that it was possible, and he could not help but think indignantly, *I* am not of Memphis, I came here only as an arm of Your compassion and I shouldn't be cut off.

God is love, we teach the children.

God is love, we preach from the pulpit.

God is love?

It was easy to see why someone who had lived beyond the tender years of youth might find the doctrine questionable. There were times, Louis supposed, when the love that was God would not bear close inspection. It was not always what one had been led to expect. He must now accept that love *on faith*, in defiance of the apparent evidence. That was how it was with every mystery, wasn't it? This is bread, this is wine. No, this is the body of Christ, this is the blood of Christ. This is death. No, this is the beginning of endless life. God is not here, not in *this* shape. You are wrong, God is here *especially* in this shape. *His bones are out of joint. We hide our faces from Him. We esteem Him not.* It is a terrifying thing to look upon Him when He is suffering. And yet this is the gaze in which His love is proven.

Perhaps an understanding of God's love could never be completely unfastened from the redemptive suffering of Christ. If God was to be worshipped at all, it would have to be from a position never too distant from the Cross. Then other horrors, by comparison, would never cause faith to be dashed. The true Christian, Louis realized, worshipped God already for the most unfair thing that had ever happened.

Yes, God was in His sanctuary—but He was also here. This was the world into which He had come, the world in which He had suffered for sins not His own, the world in which He still suffered mystically in His poor, and in His body the Church. The connection between Christ and His Church was so intimate that He had said to Saul not "Why persecutest thou my followers?" but "Why persecutest thou me?" *Me!*

It occurred to Louis, as he thought of that scene near Damascus, that he would gladly have borne persecution for the sake of Christ. Why was that not required of him instead of this? Falling victim to a filthy pestilence seemed such a meaningless, unfruitful humiliation. The buggy was transporting him—and Christ with him—into a Christianity that did not cheer the heart. And it was inconceivable that this was the "*singular* mission" Father Benson had envisioned when he sent him from Cowley St. John. There was no mission to it. But he remembered he had told the respected monk that he desired above all else a closer union with Christ. Was that why he was here? This was hardly what he'd had in mind. He drew back from the irony of it. There had to be a higher reason why everything was turning out this way.

"Why?" he asked aloud.

Dr. Dalzell stopped singing, but said nothing. His reserve hinted that he understood the question clearly.

Christ also was silent.

A bell tolled in the distance behind them. It was the only answer he was going to get—for now, at any rate—and it was not an answer at all, but a question, the same question, crying out again and again, sounding the sound for ages past and ages to come.

Louis looked at Dr. Dalzell. "St. Mary's?"

"If my ear serves me correctly, yes. I assume that Sister Thecla has departed. I'm sorry I wasn't there. But we must finish our little business, you and I, before I go back."

"*I see the Lord!*" Sister Thecla had cried that night in the upstairs hall. Now Louis heard her again. There were no arms to restrain her this time, there was no voice to deny the validity of her sight. And the turbulence of bats, against which she had fought when he tried to give her communion, had suddenly become a swarm of angels defining with motion the Perfect Stillness of the Throne of Heaven.

The bell came in waves over the earth. Strange, Louis thought, that in each wave the harshness of metal clapping metal should resolve to a mellow sonority. But that was always the character of bells. Harmonic distress and harmonic peace were knowable in the rising and tumbling of the same tone. It was interesting, since the sound that announced a death was no different from the sound that called humankind to worship. When the tolling was done and the first wave of silence came, now as always, the ear captured the timbre in its purest resonance.

Dr. Dalzell brought the buggy to a stop in front of an old structure that disgraced the intersection where it stood. The bricks were loosening and the second story appeared insecure in its saddle. In view, beyond a row of more presentable buildings and across another street, lay the square with its canopy of trees and depths of amiable shade. The park atmosphere so close by, ghostly though it was, made the infirmary all the less inviting. Louis remained in the buggy while Dr. Dalzell went inside to see if care could be arranged. He looked toward the square and tried to dream of a normal world, a world in which bands played and couples strolled. Eddies of nausea plied against the reverie, preventing him that escape, and after a time he was forced to surrender his head over the side of the buggy.

He lay on a cot beside a windowless wall.

"I am Dr. Smith," the man said to him. "Your friend has gone. You must stop calling out. We are going to do what we can for you, but you must cooperate and be quiet."

"I shall, God helping me. But there is no air."

"I didn't design the building. Nor did I choose it. It happens, however, that this is the hole I've been given for a hospital, and there is only so much space."

"I didn't mean to complain," Louis said.

"Then don't, or I'll have to remind you that we relaxed

our rules in order to take you in at all. We were set up exclusively for the care of physicians and nurses. They have come to Memphis from all over, and every day more of them are falling sick themselves. If our services are acceptable to *them*, surely *you* can adjust. We make do with what we have. At least that's how it is in a scientific profession. I presume it's the same in your business of religion. God doesn't provide *all* of your wants, am I right?''

Louis refused to speak.

''Besides, you're not on God's territory now,'' Dr. Smith said, walking off. ''I'm the boss around here.''

·15·

I AM BEING very quiet, Louis thought. I am not making a sound.

In time, the dark went darker.

Then flew one of the seraphim unto me, having a live coal in his hand, which he had taken with the tongs from the altar: And he laid it upon my mouth—

A shadow scuttled past.
"In the beginning was the smell of a slop jar."
The shadow spoke with the voice of Dr. Smith.

Purgatory, Louis thought.
Some of his brethren argued for the doctrine, others would have none of it. Louis had never been certain exactly where he should plant himself on the question. He did not find the design unthinkable in a theology of grace,

and whenever he had leaned in its direction he had thought of it as, indeed, one more *provision* of grace. He usually sided, however, with those who held that the cleansing fire had indulged itself to the full in the pain of Christ. Was the Atonement not complete and *written?* He liked to believe that the sight of God, the first quick burn of it when blindness was peeled away, would accomplish the final purification. So he had concerned himself only vaguely with purgatory as a *place*.

But here he was.

And it wasn't the classical picture at all. It seemed artistically incorrect and therefore was the worst kind of surprise. To think of this airless ward in terms of purification was impossible.

The light of morning was somewhere down the passage, too weak for a full invasion.

The light became a curse as soon as the ward took shape. Louis could see that the dream was not a dream. The wall was there, the plaster gaping. He threw his hand against the look of it. The reality of the brick inscribed itself upon his knuckles. Up and down the ward, the voices had faces and the odors had locations.

He closed his eyes.

He was in the belly of a great fish.

His cradle swam deeply through the paths of the sea.

When thou passest through the waters, I will be with thee.

A young man stood beside the cot. His sleeves were rolled and the hair on his arms lifted to a flaxen mist.

"I'm your nurse. Pay no attention to Smith. He's a bastard of the first order."

The language did not offend Louis.

Dr. Dalzell said, "Take and eat this in remembrance that Christ died for thee."

Louis choked on the solid.

Dr. Dalzell was saying, "Drink this in remembrance that Christ's blood was shed for thee, and be thankful."

"Where is the pain?" the nurse asked.

"Here."

"How long since you went?"

"I can't remember."

The nurse disappeared.

"It's watermelon tea."

"You are my friend?"

"I'm your friend. Drink it. It will help bring the urine."

"You are from God, did you know?"

"I wouldn't claim *that*, sir, but I am from God's *country*. I come from a town in North Carolina, up in the mountains. Let's take another swallow. There. That's a man. ⸳Where are you from, sir?"

"A beautiful little church in Hoboken, New Jersey." The flavor of the watermelon tea, though it was nothing to dwell on, grew more distinct and made Louis pause. "And from other points. I was born in St. Louis."

"And here we are."

"Yes. Here we are. I don't think I've ever seen you before."

"I suppose we took different routes, sir."

"I suppose that's true. We were coming from different places."

"Drink some more."

"Tell me about the mountains."

Louis listened to the young man describe the wooded mountains round about the town where he was born, how they drifted like clouds and yet were always there. The young man had an eye for the grandeur of the Lord and, in his own simple way, was an artist with words.

Louis said, "You would appreciate the magnificent old cathedrals in England."

"How is the care?"

It was Dr. Dalzell.

"I have a good nurse," Louis said.

Dr. Dalzell was keeping his word.

The great fish began to cavort. Louis wanted out. He opened his eyes and found that it wasn't night at all.

A boy tore through the ward. Behind him, tied at the end of a length of twine, slid a goose, croaking. The goose was like a kite trying to catch a wind.

Louis was up, stumbling into cots, chasing the offender for Sister Frances. She was right. The boy needed the hand of a man.

Suddenly there was no boy and no goose, and Louis was in the arms of Dr. Smith.

I am being very quiet, Louis thought. I am not making a sound.

"I remember you," Louis said, shocked and pleased. He pulled his sheet to his chin. "You're the young lady I saw on the train."

"I'm afraid not. I'm your friend from North Carolina."

"Oh."

"Let me under the sheet, sir. The whiskey will feel good."

One by one, solemn and vested, they passed by the cot—Father Benson, Father Sword, Bishop Quintard, Dr. Houghton, Dr. Tschiffely. Not a glance was cast toward Louis, and he took their disregard as a mercy. He felt that he was a poor adornment for the Gospel of Christ.

Many brave hearts are asleep in the deep, they sang.

When the procession was out of sight, they seemed to be singing from an ambulatory.

So beware, be-ware. Be-e-e-e-waaaare.

He received the Bread and the Wine.

Dr. Dalzell would answer none of his questions concerning the health of the Sisters, none directly, except to say that Sister Hughetta seemed to be pulling through.

"And the woman, Mrs. Bullock?"

Dr. Dalzell went to something else. "Mr. Schuyler,

you have a telegram from your father. Shall I read it to you?"

Louis hesitated.

"Perhaps," Dr. Dalzell said, "you would like to read it yourself. Can you see to read?"

"You—please."

"—*Your words have touched my heart. You have my full consent, and my blessing.*"

"That's like air to breathe," Louis said.

Quickened, he began to notice the members of the colony in which he lay. Here was the world in all of its need. Here were the people to whom he had been sent. Why had he shut them out of his mind? He could not restore them, he knew, but he could pour the love of Christ upon them. He could announce the unlikely story once again. *The Word became flesh and dwelt among us.* Would they believe it?

Probably not.

But that was beside the point.

The nurse was away.

Louis swaddled himself in his sheet and climbed out of the cot. His legs felt like the legs of a fresh colt. Either that or like the legs of an impaired old man, he didn't know which.

He believed in doing things decently and in order, every motion accomplishing its art and purpose in the progression of the service, but there were times when the doing was more important than the manner. He stood in the middle of the ward and, reaching out to steady himself at the pulpit that wasn't there, began to speak the verities.

He saw the devil coming toward him in the form of Dr. Smith, coming like a bull in fury, breathing hard, shaking his head and lowering to hook.

I am being very quiet, Louis thought. I am not making a sound.

"Smith's a bastard, but he's right, sir. You must stay down. He's rough and from Texas, but he's a real scientific man. You must not excite yourself. You must not excite the others. Smith knows this kind of fever and he doesn't want anybody agitated."

The pain in his abdomen made Louis cry out. His friend's hand was there in encouragement, flesh attending flesh. The water would not come.

"Sir, at least you're not vomiting. Be glad of that. Vomiting can tear a man apart."

Dr. Smith said, "Did I hear him preaching again?"
The nurse said, "He was only praying."

The arm was near.
Because the arm was near, the mountains were near.
As the mountains are round about Jerusalem, so the Lord is round about his people.

"I believe in God, the Father Almighty, Maker of heaven and earth—"

"Shhh."

"And in Jesus Christ his only Son our Lord—"

"Shhh. Not so loud. For your sake, please."

"Who was conceived by the Holy Ghost, Born of the Virgin Mary, Suffered under Pontius Pilate, was Crucified, dead and buried. He descended into hell—"

"Shhh. Smith is coming."

Louis said in a loud voice, "The third day he rose again from the dead—"

I am being very quiet, Louis thought. I am not making a sound.

"It won't be long. Take him on out to the dead-house now. Stack him with the others. If he's determined to preach to the last, let him preach to the ones he can't disturb."

"You're not serious," the nurse said.

"Don't worry. He'll be gone by the time the evening wagon comes. And that priest who calls himself a doctor won't be back until tomorrow. Our patient has *had* his holy feeding today."

"You *are* a bastard."

"I'm capable of solving problems, if that's what you mean."

"I will have nothing to do with this."

"Then stand back, I will do it myself."

Louis knew where he was.

He lay in a lean-to in the alley, his head near the open door. He had managed to uncover his face, working the sheet with movements of his fingers. He lay spent from the exertion. He tried not to strangle on the fresh air. The sun, although it softened as it fell inside the door, was so bright that he had to hold everything at a distance, through his lashes.

His travelling bag was not there.

A shadow came to the light. When Louis realized that it was the nurse who was entering the lean-to, the shadow became the light and the light became shadow.

"This is the season of strong effects," Louis said.

His habit of awe was allegiant even now.

The nurse sat down on the floor beside him, told him he was with him, told him he would not leave him.

"I know," Louis said.

Suddenly he could not imagine where he was, and then something in the atmosphere remembered itself to his pores. Was he in one of the magnificent old cathedrals in England? No. The architecture was more intimate than that.

"Tell me," he whispered, "am I in my beautiful little church in Hoboken?"

He seemed to be passing through the purest of silences. If there was an answer at all, it was somewhere behind him, fallen, unable to follow him to the altar.

♦   ♦   ♦

ADDENDUM

THE LAST SCENE of the story took place on September 17, 1878. The removal to the alley is mentioned in unpublished letters of Dr. Dalzell, who was grieved to learn that this did in fact occur.

Sister Ruth died that same afternoon. Mrs. Bullock had died the day before. Sister Frances died a few weeks later.

Sisters Clare and Hughetta survived the epidemic, along with Dean Harris and Dr. Dalzell. Sisters Flora and Helen, present at St. Mary's but not identified by name in the novel, also survived, as did Dr. White, Rector of Calvary Church, to whom Dean Harris had referred in his first conversation with Louis.

The convert (called Mr. Alberson in the novel) died of the fever. His baptism is a matter of record on the Cathedral register.

Annie Cook did not survive. (Annie Cook was the madam's real name. It is history that she turned her establishment into an infirmary. Whether or not Louis called at her Mansion House is impossible to know, but the author suspects that he did. Dr. Dalzell in several accounts told of how he warned him not to go into the "deeper" parts of town, and of how the young priest still went to every infirmary he could find.)

By the time frost came to Memphis that year, over 5,000 persons had died of yellow fever.

Three years later, in 1881, Carlos Juan Finlay, a Scottish-French physician living in Cuba, made known his belief that the mosquito was the spreader of yellow fever. But he could not prove he was correct.

In 1900, the United States Army appointed a committee to study the problem. Volunteers were exposed to mosquitos known to have bitten persons infected with yellow fever. All of the volunteers were stricken, and one of them, a doctor, died shortly afterwards. Carlos Juan Finlay's belief was confirmed: the mosquito was the villain. Yellow fever now could be battled effectively.